LOWELL LIBSON LTD
BRITISH ART

NEW YORK · ANNUAL EXHIBITION
BRITISH ART: RECENT ACQUISITIONS
at Stellan Holm · 1018 Madison Avenue
23–31 January 2015 ·

MAASTRICHT
TEFAF: THE EUROPEAN FINE ART FAIR
13–22 March 2015

LONDON
MASTERPIECE LONDON
25 June–1 July 2015

LONDON
LONDON ART WEEK
3–10 July 2015

LOWELL
LIBSON LTD
2015

LOWELL LIBSON LTD

BRITISH ART

3 Clifford Street · London w1s 2lf
Telephone: +44 (0)20 7734 8686
Fax: +44 (0)20 7734 9997
Email: pictures@lowell-libson.com
Website: www.lowell-libson.com

The gallery is open by appointment, Monday to Friday
The entrance is in Old Burlington Street

Lowell Libson   *lowell@lowell-libson.com*

Deborah Greenhalgh   *deborah@lowell-libson.com*

Jonny Yarker   *jonny@lowell-libson.com*

Cressida St Aubyn   *cressida@lowell-libson.com*

Published by Lowell Libson Limited 2015
Text and publication © Lowell Libson Limited
All rights reserved
ISBN 978 0 9929096 0 4

Designed and typeset in Dante by Dalrymple
Photography by Rodney Todd-White & Son Ltd
Colour reproduction by Altaimage
Printed in Belgium by Albe De Coker

Cover: a sheet of 18th-century Italian
paste paper (collection: Lowell Libson)

Frontispiece: detail from
William Turner of Oxford 1782–1862
The Sands at Barmouth, North Wales
see pages 116–119

Overleaf: detail from
John Robert Cozens 1752–1799, *An Alpine
Landscape, near Grindelwald, Switzerland*
see pages 31–33

INDEX OF ARTISTS

FOREWORD

THIS CATALOGUE OF OUR RECENT ACQUISITIONS IS CERTAINLY longer than its predecessors and, to my mind, it is also unquestionably richer in its contents. We have been fortunate in being able to gather together some exceptional works of great beauty, extreme rarity and historical importance, a number of which have emerged onto the market after long periods of obscurity.

It is a great privilege to be able to offer extraordinary paintings by both William Blake and Samuel Palmer. The beguiling tempera of *The Virgin hushing the infant John the Baptist* of 1799 is one of Blake's best preserved paintings and was possibly the first work by the artist to enter a North American collection. It is serendipitous to be able to show it with Palmer's wonderful *Landscape – Twilight* of c.1830. This luminous Shoreham period work is perhaps Palmer's most beautiful oil and has remained, uncleaned and in the same family collection since about 1890.

Another remarkable re-emergence is Joshua Reynolds's emotionally charged *Dionysius Areopagite*. This painting, only known to art historians on the basis of a rare print, shows Reynolds at his most serious and painterly at the moment when he was trying to shape a new and elevated British School of painting as first President of the recently formed Royal Academy. The model for this 'Disciple of St Paul' was George White, a street mender, and here we see Reynolds looking towards Rembrandt for guidance.

As usual we have gathered an interesting group of portraits, the earliest of which is a fascinating 1730s pastel by Arthur Pond of a female amateur artist at her easel. Pastels are further represented by lovely and characteristic examples by Gardner and Hamilton. Copley's most elaborate drawing; a study for the important group of the Pepperrell family was acquired by us from a descendant of the artist and although recently sold, we include it here. A complex and masterly drawing by Rowlandson comprising a compendium of heads of his favourite 'types' and the most impressive of Romney's studies for his masterpiece of the Gower Children round off the eighteenth century.

Nineteenth-century portraiture is represented by an interesting group of drawings, which came to us individually by chance over the year, depicting the quartet of Queen Victoria, Talleyrand, Paganini and Chopin. The undoubted star of our portrait drawings this year is Sir Thomas Lawrence's superb drawing of the Wellesley-Pole sisters. Executed in 1814, almost certainly at the behest of the Duke of Wellington, the girls' uncle, this drawing is perhaps the most sophisticated and elaborate of his career.

Landscape art is very strongly represented, aside of the Palmer, by impressive and beautiful examples of the work of Gainsborough, Jones, Cozens, Constable and Turner. The very large Constable oil study of 1816 is here published for the first time by Anne Lyles and it has been fascinating to spend time with it during the run of the Victoria & Albert Museum's beautiful Constable exhibition. Likewise, the Late Turner show at Tate has further illuminated for me the remarkable fluency of our hugely accomplished and captivating 1836 *plein air* watercolour of the Alps near Chambéry. I am very grateful to William Vaughan, Anne Lyles and Ian Warrell who have written fascinating catalogue entries on the Palmer, Constable and Turner.

I have always been fascinated by the history of the art trade and we have been fortunate in acquiring two compelling portraits of the greatest of nineteenth-century art dealers. Sir William Agnew, hugely charismatic and perspicacious, transformed the international art market in the late nineteenth century and his portraits by Frank Holl and Edward Onslow Ford give a real sense of the astuteness, determination and good humour that propelled him to pre-eminence in his profession.

We always seem to include one work that many might think of being uncharacteristic of our usual interests. This year that accolade will probably be given to the large and masterly drawing of the late 1950s by John Bratby. This is a drawing that I have admired for over twenty years and which I believe absolutely encapsulates that moment of rebellion and reinvention in post-war society.

I am deeply indebted to my colleagues on very many fronts. Jonny Yarker is entirely responsible for the catalogue entries (other than the three mentioned above) and has coped well with my frequent well-meant suggestions. The excellence of the notes bear testament to his many talents. Jonny's remarkable knowledge, keen curiosity and excellent eye continue to amaze and he has made a significant contribution to the business since he joined us two years ago. As usual, Laurence Allan has been responsible for the high standard of framing and the hanging of our various shows. Deborah Greenhalgh and Cressida St Aubyn, who has recently joined us, are a back-up duo of incomparable efficiency and tremendous good humour and they keep the entire show on the road.

We all hope to see our many friends over the coming year either at the gallery in London or when we are exhibiting in New York and at Maastricht.

LOWELL LIBSON

ARTHUR POND 1701–1758

An Amateur Pastellist at her Easel

Pastel
25 × 20 inches · 640 × 508 mm
Drawn c.1737
In the original Japanned frame

Arthur Pond
Rhoda (née Delaval), Lady Astley, c.1750
Oil on canvas · 30¼ × 27 inches · 768 × 686 mm
© National Portrait Gallery, London
Given by Montague Bernard, 1979

The present portrait is a rare image of a female pastellist at work executed during the early eighteenth century. Comparable to the portrait of the amateur draughtswoman Rhoda Delaval, also by Arthur Pond in the National Portrait Gallery, it probably shows an aristocratic amateur at work. During the 1730s and 1740s pastel or 'crayons' became a hugely popular medium amongst an intimate circle of patrician women, and Pond, who was already by this date a successful portraitist in the medium, became the most fashionable tutor in London. Whilst the sitter of the present portrait cannot be identified with total certainty a number of circumstantial clues point towards Lady Helena Perceval (1714–1746), the daughter of the Anglo-Irish statesman and intellectual John Perceval, 1st Earl of Egmont, who was a talented draughtswoman and is recorded sitting to Pond in 1737.[1] Whilst this identification may not be entirely secure, the present compelling portrait stands as a representation of a highly significant moment of female, amateur creativity in a circle of aristocratic friends with court connections either to George II and Queen Caroline or Frederick and Augusta, Prince and Princess of Wales. This catalogue entry will trace this circle of female artists and underline the significance of the present portrait as illustrative of an influential moment of activity.

Pond's artistic education may have begun under the portrait painter John Vanderbank, whose name appears near Pond's in the first subscription list of the St Martin's Lane Academy, founded in 1720. There Pond must have met William Hogarth and the painter George Knapton, probable source of a crucial introduction to Jonathan Richardson senior, portrait painter,

author, and art theorist, whose books were published by John and Paul Knapton. Pond began his career as a portrait painter in oil, but rapidly diversified into print making and art dealing. His surviving journal reveals the networks of his patronage and the full range of activities he was involved in by 1734, which included a burgeoning career as a pastel portraitist.

Pastel portraiture became fashionable during the 1730s. The engraver and antiquarian recorded in his notebooks:
Crayon painting has met with so much encouragement of late years here. that several Painters those that had been in Italy to study, as Knapton Pond Hoare &c for the practice of painting in Oyl. found at their return that they could not make any extraordinary matter of it, turned to painting in Crayons and several made great advantage of it. It looking pleasant and coverd with a glass large Gold Frames was much commended. for novelty.[2]

Arthur Pond returned from his Grand Tour in 1727 and rapidly established himself as a pastel portraitist of some celebrity. As Louise Lippincott has pointed out, from 1734 to 1737 Pond's annual income rose rapidly with profits amounting to £280 in 1738.[3] This was largely due to the new fashion for pastel portraits and Pond attracted significant clientele including members of the court. But it was probably not Pond's portraiture alone which recommended him to amateur artists. In Italy Pond evidently encountered the works of the celebrated Venetian pastellist, Rosalaba Carriera; once back in London he capitalised on this association, specialising in copies of Carriera's works, particularly the celebrated *Four Seasons*. Pond produced copies of the *Four Seasons* for the collector Peter Delmé in 1738 for £64 and

John Faber, the Younger, after J. Wills
Lady Helena Rawdon, 1745
Mezzotint · 6 × 4 inches · 152 × 102 mm
© The Trustees of the British Museum

Mary Delany
Lady Catherine Hamner
Pencil
The Lilly Library, Bloomington, Indiana

[10]

the following year he sold a set to another noted collector, Sir William Morice of Werrington.[4] Carriera's fame, her status as a woman artist, and the attractive, decorative compositions – four young women holding the emblems of each season – made them frequent subjects of amateur copyists.

As has been frequently observed 'crayons' or pastels were less time consuming than oils, easier to use and less messy in application, making them ideal for amateurs, whilst their intense colours and versatility made them an attractive and highly decorative accomplishment to master. The first significant female pupil we know Pond had was Grace Carteret, Countess of Dysart. Her cousin, Mary Pendarves, more famously known by her second married name, Delany, and celebrated as one of the most significant amateur artists of the eighteenth century for her paper collages of botanical specimens, gave an account of her training under Pond.[5] Writing to her sister in June 1734 Mary Pendarves noted:

Lady Dysart goes on extremely well with her drawing; she has got to crayons, and I design to fall into that way. I hope Mr Pond will help me too, for his colouring in crayons I think the best I have seen of an English painter – it tries my eyes less than [needle]work, and entertains me better; I aim at everything, and will send you a sample of what I am about, but I don't design to colour till I am more perfect in my drawing.[6]

Dysart's surviving pastels show that she was a proficient copyist.[7] Mary Pendarves does seem to have received 'help' from Pond as well, although there are no specific payments for lessons in his surviving account book, a number of entries suggest that she was receiving both tuition and supplies from him. Pond supplied her with pastels, noting

in 1735 the receipt of 1 guinea from 'Mrs Pendarvis for french Crayons'.[8] At the same time Pond was producing portraits of her friends and relations; Mary Pendarvis's close friend and life-long correspondent Margaret Bentinck, Duchess of Portland commissioned a portrait of Catherine Dashwood. This in-turn led to a number of fashionable commissions from figures associated with the court, including portraits of Henrietta, Countess of Pomfret and Frances, Countess of Hertford, both ladies of the bedchamber, and Anne Vane, maid of honour to Queen Caroline.[9] Pond also drew portraits of Princess Mary and Princess Louisa, daughters of George II and a number of members of Frederick, Prince of Wale's household.[10]

In the midst of this fashionable circle was Lady Helena Percival, daughter of John Perceval, 1st Earl of Egmont. She was a noted amateur artist who had trained initially with Bernard Lens III.[11] A landscape drawing dated 1737 in the British Museum shows her early debt to Lens and his topographical work but also her skill as an artist.[12] In March 1736 Egmont recorded in his diary visiting Pond's studio in Great Queen Street: 'This morning I went to Mr. Pond, the painter in Queen Street, to see my daughter Helena sit to him for her picture in crayons. I met my daughter-in-law Percival there, who promised she would sit for me also.'[13] In August Perceval praised the portrait as 'a fine piece and like': could this be referring to this pastel? The present portrait certainly appears close physically to Lady Helena, who was painted by James Wills in the mid-1740s shortly after her marriage to Sir John Rawdon. In the engraving of Wills's portrait, Helena Rawdon shares the same almond shaped eyes, elongated nose and similarly dressed hair as the woman in the present portrait, although it is dangerous to make too much of this similarity given the generalising fashion of portraiture of the period.[14]

Another amateur who began with lessons under Bernard Lens but then progressed to Pond was Mary Pendarves. We know from Pond's journal that he continued to supply her with materials after her marriage to Dean Delany and move to Dublin.[15] Although Mary Delany is most associated with the cut paperwork she undertook as a widow in later life, it is clear from her correspondence that pastel was a medium she greatly enjoyed and by 1740 was proficient enough to produce a copy of Rosalba Carriera's self-portrait. It was a work seen and admired by George Vertue who noted: 'at Madam Pendarvis. who draws & paints in Crayons very well...several Copies of this Lady painting in Crayons from fine Italian paintings well copied – the portrait Rosalba the famous limner & crayon painter in her Time.'[16] Her will records a number of pastel copies which give an idea of the breadth and ambition of female copyists at this date: works by Rosalba – including a copy of *Summer*, one of the *Four Seasons* – and old masters including two Holy Families by Francesco Trevisani and works by Guido Reni and Veronese.[17]

Turning to the portrait itself, it represents an outstanding image of an amateur at work. Pond produced one further portrait in this mode, an oil of his most celebrated pupil, Rhoda Delaval, which is preserved in the National Portrait Gallery; it shows Delaval at work but was painted later than the present work in about 1750 and is in oil rather than pastel. The present

portrait provides instructive insight into the process of executing a pastel in the period. A number of eighteenth-century accounts and manuals explaining pastel painting survive, most famously in John Russell's treatise, which was in effect a handbook to the art of pastel painting. He revised and enlarged it in 1777, and it remained popular throughout the nineteenth century. Russell's *Elements of Painting with Crayons* gives a remarkable explication of the working methods of British pastellists.[18] As is visible in the portrait he recommended a strong blue paper, the thicker the better and mounted on linen; he advised students to paint seated, 'with the box of crayons in his lap', adding 'let the windows of the room where he paints be darkened, at least to the height of six feet.'[19] The smudging or *sfumato* effect Russell described as 'sweetening with the finger', although this was to be used only as a base, the final marks were to be applied with a sharpened pastel to add precision and clarity to his sitter's features. Russell describes the stage depicted in Pond's portrait: 'When the Head is brought to some degree of forwardness, let the Back-ground be laid in, which must be treated in a different manner, covering it as thin as possible, and rubbing it into the paper with a Leather-stump.'[20]

It seems likely that Lady Helena, who was already a talented draughtsman, received some form of tuition from Pond at the same time as sitting to him for her portrait. The head of the child that features in the portrait could well be one of the unmarried Lady Helena's nephews, in which may explain the presence of her sister-in-law, Lady Catherine Cecil, at her sitting as recorded by the Earl of Egmont. In their circle, exchanging

Attributed to Lady Helena Perceval after Rosalba Carriera *Summer*
Pastel · 25 × 20 inches · 635 × 508 mm
Lowell Libson Ltd

Attributed to Lady Helena Perceval after Rosalba Carriera *Winter*
Pastel · 25 × 20 inches · 635 × 508 mm
Lowell Libson Ltd

works of art in the form of portraits, copies, caricatures and landscapes was extremely common as an expression of friendship and intimacy. An album of drawings by amateurs from Mary Delany's circle preserved in the Lily Library in Indiana contains a drawing, possibly by Mary Delany herself, of Lady Helena's sister, Lady Catherine Hanmer at an easel apparently working in pastel.[21] Whilst no helpful early provenance for the present portrait is known it is accompanied by three pastel copies probably by the sitter depicted in our portrait by Pond. The four pastels are all framed in identical, japanned, black and gilt frames, which are similar to frames used by the Irish ornithological painter Samuel Dixon. Two of the copies have hanging instructions in an eighteenth-century hand on the reverse, suggesting the four pastels formed part of a decorative scheme at some point. Two of the copies are after two of Rosalba Carriera's *Four Seasons – Winter* and *Summer* – adding weight to the theory that they are the product of one of Pond's amateur pastellists.

Pond's portrait is a compelling image of an amateur pastellist at work, drawn at a moment when the medium was being practiced by a group of fashionable and well-connected aristocratic women. Whilst firm identification of the sitter remains allusive, the references to Pond's portrait of Lady Helena Perceval, her ability as an artist and the striking physical likeness offers one possibility. Lady Helena Perceval was at the heart of a group of women who were keen amateur pastellists who took lessons from Pond and practiced at the highest level, drawing each other and exchanging portraits and copies of old masters as signs of their friendship and accomplishment. This

remarkable image and its associated works offer a remarkable insight into the world of eighteenth-century female amateur art.

We are extremely grateful to Clarissa Campbell Orr, Mary Delany's biographer, and Neil Jeffares for their help in preparing this note.

NOTES

1 Ed. Louise Lippincott, 'Arthur Pond's Journal of Receipts and Expenses, 1734–1750', *The Walpole Society*, LIV, 1988, p.237.

2 G. Vertue, eds. L. Cust and A. Hind, 'The Notebooks of George Vertue', *The Walpole Society,* London, 1929–47, III, p.109.

3 Louise Lippincott, *Selling Art in Georgian London*, New Haven and London, 1983, p.81.

4 Ed. Louise Lippincott, 'Arthur Pond's Journal of Receipts and Expenses, 1734–1750', *The Walpole Society*, LIV, 1988, p.239 and p.250.

5 Ed. Mark Laird and Alicia Weisberg-Roberts, *Mary Delaney and her Circle*, exh.cat. New Haven (Yale Center for British Art), 2010.

6 Ed. Lady Llanover, *The Autobiography and correspondence of Mary Granville, Mary Delany: with interesting reminiscences of King George the Third and Queen Charlotte*, London, 1861, I, p.485.

7 Neil Jeffares, *Dictionary of Pastellists before 1800*, London, 2006, pp.176–177. She is recorded sitting to Pond for her portrait in 1740, see Ed. Louise Lippincott, 'Arthur Pond's Journal of Receipts and Expenses, 1734–1750', *The Walpole Society*, LIV, 1988, p.252. Lady Dysart possibly gave this portrait to Mary Delany, as she left a portrait of 'Lady Dysart, Lord Granville's daughter, by Pond (crayons)' in her will to

her nephew 'Mr J. Dewes'. See Ed. Lady Llanover, *The Autobiography and correspondence of Mary Granville, Mary Delany: with interesting reminiscences of King George the Third and Queen Charlotte*, London, 1861, III, p.485.

8 Louise Lippincott, 'Arthur Pond's Journal of Receipts and Expenses, 1734–1750', *The Walpole Society*, London, 1988, LIV, p.227.

9 Louis Lippincott, *Selling Art in Georgian London*, New Haven and London, 1983, p.40.

10 Louis Lippincott, *Selling Art in Georgian London*, New Haven and London, 1983, p.40.

11 The Earl of Egmont noted in 1732: 'went to see the works of Mr Lens, limner to the King, and enamel painter, who teaches my daughter Helena to draw, and afterwards to see Zeaman's paintings in St Martin's Lane.' Ed. R.A. Roberts, *Royal Manuscripts Commission, Report on the Manuscripts of the Earl of Egmont*, London, 1920, I, p.257.

12 See Kim Sloan, '*A Noble Art': Amateur Artists and Drawing Masters c.1600–1800*, exh.cat. London (British Museum, 2000, no.44, p.70.

13 Ed. R.A. Roberts, *Royal Manuscripts Commission, Report on the Manuscripts of the Earl of Egmont*, London, 1920, II, p.364.

14 For another portrait of Helena Rawdon see ed. Alastair Laing, *Clerics and Connoisseurs: An Irish Art Collection Through three Centuries*, exh. cat. London (Kenwood House), 2002, no.4.

15 Ed. R.A. Roberts, *Royal Manuscripts Commission, Report on the Manuscripts of the Earl of Egmont*, London, 1920, I, p.257.

16 G. Vertue, eds. L. Cust and A. Hind, 'The Notebooks of George Vertue', *The Walpole Society,* London, 1929–47, IV, p.177.

17 For a list of Mrs Delany's pastels see Neil Jeffares, *Dictionary of Pastellists before 1800*, online edition.

18 J. Russell, Elements of Painting with Crayons, London, 1772, p.ii.

19 J. Russell, Elements of Painting with Crayons, London, 1772, p.21.

20 J. Russell, Elements of Painting with Crayons, London, 1772, p.25.

21 Other drawings in the album were made by the Earl of Egmont, Lady Helena Perceval and Lady Catherine Hanmer's father. I am extremely grateful to Clarissa Campbell Orr for drawing my attention to this album.

THOMAS GAINSBOROUGH RA 1727–1788

An open landscape with resting drovers

Thinned oil paint and watercolour with white lead on paper prepared with a red ground, varnished
15¾ × 20¼ inches · 400 × 514 mm
Painted early 1770s

COLLECTIONS
Private collection, 1980;
Phillips, 11th November 1980, lot 61;
Private collection, London, acquired at the above sale, to 1998;
Private collection, USA, 2014.

LITERATURE
John Hayes, 'Gainsborough Drawings: A Supplement to the Catalogue Raisonné', *Master Drawings*, vol.XXI, no.4, 1983, no.924; Hugh Belsey, 'A Second Supplement to John Hayes's The Drawings of Thomas Gainsborough', *Master Drawings*, vol.XLVI, no.4, 2008, no.924.

EXHIBITED
London, Anthony Dallas & Son Ltd, 1983, no.1 (on loan);
London, Spink-Leger, *Master Drawings 17th to 20th Century*, 1998, no.15.

Thomas Gainsborough
Rocky landscape with cattle, 1770–75
Black chalk, watercolour and oil, varnished
8⅜ × 12 inches · 213 × 306 mm
© The Trustees of the British Museum

This refined varnished mixed-media drawing was made by Gainsborough at Bath in the early 1770s; an experimental process, these rapidly worked, highly evocative sheets underline Gainsborough's deeply personal engagement with the processes of landscape drawing. These drawings also acted as vehicles for his experimentation with both techniques and materials. The method used in this particular drawing was outlined in a letter which gives a sense of his innovation. In the present drawing Gainsborough has matched technical invention with a novelty of approach, in the present sheet Gainsborough has created an almost abstract composition, where abbreviated forms are used to suggest an open landscape under an open sky. We know from contemporaries that these ambiguous drawings, devoid of specific narrative, were highly prized by collectors and keenly discussed as works imbued with feeling. This large, varnished sheet, belongs to a particularly important and well documented group of Gainsborough's landscape drawings and is an unusually bold and attractive example.

Gainsborough's own description of producing varnished drawings such as this, is contained in a letter dated 29 January 1773 written to his friend William Jackson. Jackson, an amateur landscape painter himself, had evidently asked for the method Gainsborough used to produce such varnished drawings. Gainsborough warned him that: 'There is no Man living that you can mentions (besides your self and one more, living) that shall ever know my secret of making those studies you mention.'[1] He then explained:

… take half a sheet of blotting paper such as the Clerks and those that keep books put upon writing instead of sand; 'tis a spongy purple paper. Paste that and half a sheet of white paper, of the same size, together, let them dry, and in that state keep them for use – take a Frame of deal about two Inches larger every way, and paste, or glue, a few sheets of very large substantial paper, no matter what sort, thick brown, blue, or any; then cut out a square half an inch less than the size of your papers for Drawing; so that it may serve for a perpetual stretching Frame or your Drawings; that is to say after you have dip't your drawings as I shall by & by direct in a liquid, in that wet state you are to take, and run some hot glue and with a brush run round the border of your stretcher, gluing about half an Inch broad which is to receive your half an Inch extraordinary allow'd for the purpose in your drawing paper, so that when that dries, it may be like a drum. Now before you do any thing by way of stretching, make the black & white of your drawing, the Effect I mean, &disposition in rough, Indian Ink shaddows & your lights of Bristol made white lead which you buy in lumps at any house painters; saw it the size you want for your white chalk, the Bristol is harder and more the temper of chalk than the London. When you see your Effect, dip it all over in skim'd milk; put it wet on [your] Frame (just glued as before observed to) let it dry, and then you correct your [illegible] with Indian Ink & if you want to add more lights, or other, do it and dip again, till all your Effect is to your mind; then tinge in your greens your browns with sap green & Bistre, your yellows with Gall stone & blues with fine Indigo.[2]

Gainsborough finally observed: 'varnish it 3 times with Spirit Varnish such as I sent you; though only Mastic & Venice Turpinetine is sufficient, then cut out your drawing but observe it must be Varnished both sides to keep it flat.'

The present sheet, probably made in about 1772, precisely represents this process. The letter is remarkable because it suggests both Gainsborough's level of inventiveness, awareness of materials – note his use of paper not designed for drawing – and pursuit of innovative techniques to create novel effects in his landscape compositions. Gainsborough has used a rich brown paper and then built up the composition, first adding the lead white, to lay in the cattle, seated figures and the suggestion of the landscape and tree. As the letter suggests this was not chalk, technical analysis undertaken by Jonathan Derow of other varnished drawings has proved that it was dry white pigment, consistent with the Bristol lead white mentioned by Gainsborough.[3] The drawing could then be dipped in milk and washes applied to build up the landscape. This gradual process can been seen in the two most distant cows, whilst the white lead highlights repel washes, the bodies are ink, allowing the different washes in the background to remain visible. Gainsborough has used a deep bistre wash to give depth to the landscape. Whilst the drawing is in outstanding condition, the fugitive nature of 'fine Indigo' means that the blues of the sky have faded.

The motif of the drawing – herdsmen and cattle – is typical of Gainsborough's landscape drawings and raises the question of its appeal to contemporaries. His varnished sheets – some measuring over a metre in length – occupied an unusual place in Gainsborough's extensive oeuvre, being, as he stated, prepared for exhibition at the Royal Academy. Whilst the present stark composition seems unlikely to have been prepared with exhibition in mind, its size and subject matter suggest that it might be one of those sent to London 'by Zoffani' which Gainsborough produced 'as they run off so quick.'[4] The appeal of these works

lay in part in their relationship with Dutch seventeenth-century landscapes. From early in his youth Gainsborough had been fascinated by the works of Salomon van Ruysdael, Aelbert Cuyp and Jan van Goyen; the muted palette and simple arrangement of cattle in an open landscape particularly recalls fashionable Dutch prototypes. But there is also evidence that contemporaries read something more immediate and emotional in Gainsborough's landscapes. The mood of such drawings was well described by Edward Edwards in his *Anecdotes of Painters*: 'in his latter works, bold effect, great breadth of form, with little variety of parts, united by a judicious management of light and shade, combine to produce a certain degree of solemnity. This solemnity, though striking, is not easily accounted for, when the simplicity of materials is considered, which seldom represent more than a stony bank, with a few trees, a pond, and some distant hills.'[5] It was this imperceptible feeling of 'solemnity' which probably explained the success of a sheet such as this. There is growing evidence that Gainsborough, in common with his contemporaries, such as Alexander Cozens, was conscious of the ability for his landscape drawings to suggest certain emotions.

This varnished drawing should be regarded as an exceptional work, not only within Gainsborough's *oeuvre*, but in our understanding of the development of landscape drawing in Britain during the eighteenth century. In the present sheet Gainsborough combines the simple compositional motifs learnt from Dutch seventeenth-century painters with an emotional ambiguity which would become central to the art of Romanticism.

Thomas Gainsborough
An Imaginary Wooded Village with Drovers and Cattle, 1771–2
Oil and mixed media on paper on canvas
24½ × 29⅜ inches · 622 × 746 mm
Yale Center for British Art, Paul Mellon Collection

NOTES

1 Ed. John Hayes, *The Letters of Thomas Gainsborough*, New Haven and London, 2001, p.110.

2 Ed. John Hayes, *The Letters of Thomas Gainsborough*, New Haven and London, 2001, pp.110–111.

3 Jonathan Derow, 'Gainsborough's Varnished Watercolour Technique', *Master Drawings*, vol.26, no.3, 1988, pp.259–71.

4 Gainsborough showed two large varnished landscapes at the Academy in 1772, traditionally identified as the 'Cartoon' now at Buscot Park and the large drawing at Yale; but the same year he also showed: 'Eight landscapes, drawings, in imitation of oil painting.' For the mention of Johan Zoffany couriering drawings from Bath to London see John Hayes, p.94.

5 Edward Edwards, *Anecdotes of Painting*, London, 1808, p.139.

SIR JOSHUA REYNOLDS PRA 1723–1792

Dionysius Areopagite, a Nobleman of Athens and Disciple of St Paul

Isaac Jehner, after Reynolds
Dionysius Areopagita
Mezzotint · Published 15 November 1776
10 × 7⅝ inches · 254 × 193 mm
© The Trustees of the British Museum

Oil on canvas
30 × 25 inches · 763 × 635 mm
Painted *c.*1772

COLLECTIONS
John Bentley, Birch House, Lancashire by 1850;
Bentley sale, Christie's, 15 May 1886, lot 67;
M. Trollope, West Bilney Hall, East Winch, Norfolk;
and by descent to 2014.

LITERATURE
E.A. Hamilton, *Catalogue Raisonné of the Engraved Works of Sir Joshua Reynolds from 1755 to 1822*, London, 1874, p.111;
Algernon Graves and W.V. Cronin, *A History of the Works of Sir Joshua Reynolds*, London, 1901, vol.IV, pp.1149–50;
Martin Postle, 'Patriarchs, prophets, and paviours: Reynolds's images of old age', *The Burlington Magazine*, 1988, vol.cxxx, pp.736–37;
Martin Postle, 'Pathos personified', *Country Life*, June 1988, p.204;
Ilaria Bignamini and Martin Postle, *The Artist's Model: its role in British Art from Lely to Etty*, exh. cat. Nottingham (University Art Gallery), 1991, pp.80–81, no.71;
Martin Postle, *Sir Joshua Reynolds: the subject pictures*, Cambridge, 1995, pp.125–126;
David Mannings and Martin Postle, *Sir Joshua Reynolds: A Complete Catalogue of his Paintings*, New Haven and London, 2000, no.2066, p.528 (as untraced);
To be published by Martin Postle in a forthcoming *Burlington Magazine* article.

EXHIBITED
British Institution, 1850, no.55 as *Dionysius the Areopagite*, (lent by John Bentley).

ENGRAVED
Isaac Jehner, as *Dionysius Areopagita, a Nobleman of Athens and Disciple of St Paul*, in mezzotint, published 15 November, 1776.

This rediscovered masterpiece is one of the most significant additions to Reynolds's *oeuvre* in recent years. Long known about from a contemporary engraving by Isaac Jehner, the painting has been untraced since 1905.[1] Dating from about 1772, the canvas belongs to an important group of pictures depicting Reynolds's favourite model, the paviour George White, the most famous of which is Reynolds's 1773 *Ugolino and his Children* (Knole House). Made shortly after the foundation of the Royal Academy the painting is a fascinating distillation of Reynolds's ambitions as a history painter. Entitled on the engraving *Dionysius Areopagita* Reynolds transforms White, a humble labourer, into a disciple of St Paul.

In 1768 the foundation of the Royal Academy saw Reynolds emerge as the preeminent painter in Britain and the Academy's first President. Conscious of his position as a society portraitist, Reynolds was keen to promote himself as a history painter and the Academy as the natural incubator of British history painting. This took the form of a series of paintings of historical and literary subjects Reynolds exhibited at the Academy and in the *Discourses* he delivered annually and in which he laid out a programmatised system of study which would prepare the young painter to become a history painter. The first fully fledged historical work Reynolds exhibited at the Academy was *Ugolino and his Children* which was also the culmination of Reynolds's relationship with George White.

George White was one of the most celebrated models in eighteenth-century London. According to the painter Joseph Moser:

Old George…owed the ease in which he passed his latter days, in a great measure to Sir Joshua Reynolds, who found him exerting himself in the laborious employment of thumping down stones in the street; and observing not only the grand and majestic traits of his countenance, but the dignity of his muscular figure, took him out of a situation to which his strength was by no means equal, clothed, fed, and had him, first as a model in his own painting room, then introduced him as a subject for the students of the Royal Academy.[2]

As Martin Postle has pointed out, whilst characterful studies of old men posed as biblical figures, prophets or saints by Continental old masters were readily available on the art market – Reynolds himself had copied a head of *Joab* by Federico Bencovich in the collection of his friend and patron, Lord Palmerston – finding a model in Britain from whom to execute a painting was more difficult.[3] White therefore offered a rare opportunity for Reynolds to combine portraiture and history painting, by painting a model in the guise of an historical or literary character. Having been discovered, possibly by the physician John Hunter in St George's Hospital, White became an important model sitting to Reynolds for a number of paintings, both private studies and public exhibition works.[4]

In 1771 Reynolds showed at the Royal Academy a picture of White entitled *Resignation*. The grand work shows White seated against a classical pillar in emulation of Titian or Van Dyck. It was engraved in 1772 and accompanied by a stanza from Oliver Goldsmith's *Deserted Village*, implying a literary context to what is essentially a portrait. In his annotated Royal Academy catalogue, Horace Walpole noted: 'This

was an old beggar, who had so fine a head that Sir Joshua chose him for the father in his picture from Dante, and painted him several times, as did others in imitation of Reynolds. There were even cameos and busts of him.' As Martin Postle has pointed out White sat to, amongst others, John Russell, Johan Zoffany, John Sanders and the sculptor John Bacon.[5] Contemporary evidence suggests that Reynolds began studies of White without a specific subject-matter in mind. His pupil, James Northcote, described the gestation of the *Ugolino* suggesting Reynolds initially painted the head-study of White and then decided to add to the canvas to create the finished composition.[6] Whilst Martin Postle has pointed out that Reynolds was planning to paint the scene from Dante from early 1770. The additions to the existing *Ugolino* confirms that Reynolds began this study without a specific narrative in mind.[7]

It is therefore likely that the present painting begun as a life-study, probably in around 1772, when Reynolds's account books record a number of sittings with 'George White bgr.', and only later acquired its title and biblical association. Although not exhibited at the Royal Academy it was engraved by Isaac Jehner in 1776 with the title 'Dionysius Areopagita: A Nobleman of Athens & Disciple of St Paul'. This title is likely to have been added by Reynolds after the picture's completion. Other depictions of White were untitled (Tate Gallery, London), given vague titles such as *Resignation* or even humourous titles, such as *Pope Pavarious* (Guildhall Art Gallery, London) a pun on White's profession as a street mender. The unusual title of the present picture may point towards a specific art historical context. Dionysius

Areopagite, a disciple of St Paul, was the subject of the most famous painting in Britain in the eighteenth century: Raphael's *St Paul Preaching in Athens* one of the Tapestry Cartoons then housed at Hampton Court. Jonathan Richardson, in his 1715 *Theory of Painting*, had particularly commended Raphael's depiction of St Paul and the audience:
the different sentiments of his auditors are as finely express'd; some appear to be angry within themselves, or with one another; and One especially is apparently Convinc'd. These last are the Free-Thinkers of that Time.[8]

Indeed it is probable that Reynolds, whilst contemplating his new role as both history painter and art theorist, had returned to Richardson's writings. The story of Ugolino and his sons had been memorably described by Richardson in his 1719 *Two Discourses*, suggesting that he was actively using Richardson's writing as a source of inspiration. Reynolds undoubtedly saw in Raphael's bearded, elderly spectators of St Paul's sermon possible source material for his own historical work.

Reynolds's approach is decidedly painterly and suggests his enduring interest in the works of Rembrandt. Reynolds owned a number of paintings by Rembrandt.[9] Amongst the autograph examples is an impressive painting of *St Bartholomew* from 1657, now in the Timken Museum in San Diego, which Reynolds acquired in 1757 from the connoisseur and collector Dr Bragge; it had previously belonged to Jonathan Richardson himself.[10] The single figure, seated in a dark interior and dramatically lit from above is highly suggestive when considering Reynolds's treatment of George White in *Dionysius Areopagite*.

Sir Joshua Reynolds
Pope Pavarius, c.1770–5
Oil on canvas · 30 × 25 inches · 762 × 635 mm
Guildhall Art Gallery, City of London

Rembrandt Harmensz. van Rijn
Saint Bartholomew, 1657
Oil on canvas · 48⅜ × 39¼ inches · 1227 × 997 mm
The Putnam Foundation, Timken Museum of Art, San Diego

Throughout the 1650s Rembrandt produced a number of characterful paintings of male saints, usually stripped of extraneous narrative detail, the paintings act as intense psychological portraits of his models, an approach which had obvious appeal to the master portraitist Reynolds. But even more than the subject-matter, it was Rembrandt's fluid, painterly technique in pictures such as *St Bartholomew* which impacted upon Reynolds's work. The dramatic, dark palette, the bold, broad application of paint and the almost haphazard application of highlights were all features Reynolds studied and emulated. Rembrandt's approach was clearly one Reynolds had considered carefully, writing in the *Twelfth Discourse* Reynolds noted that:

Rembrandt, in order to take the advantage of accident, appears often to have used the pallet-knife to lay his colours on the canvass instead of the pencil. Whether it is the knife of any other instrument, it suffices, if it is something that does not follow exactly the will. Accident in the hands of an artist who knows how to take the advantage of its hints, will often produce bold and capricious beauties of handling and facility, such as he would not have thought of, or ventured, with his pencil, under the regular restraint of his hand.[11]

In *Dionysius Areopagite* Reynolds adopts a consciously dark palette, unusual in his portraiture, and a particularly loose handling of paint. In certain areas it is possible to detect precisely this use of a palette knife and utilisation of 'accidents' to produce a 'bold and capricious' handling. White's hair is thickly painted with impasto which is consistent with the use of a palette knife. Elsewhere Reynolds has used a loaded brush to convey a sense of spontaneity: for example the serpentine line defining White's shoulder. Reynolds has also added thick, dry highlights at the end of the painting process, consistent with Rembrandt's method, particularly the scumbled line of highlight on the sleeve of the right hand. But perhaps the most Rembrandtian touch is the dramatic light which illuminates White's face.

Reynolds was not only concerned with emulating the style and approach of the old masters he was passionately keen to revive certain lost techniques. Technical analysis has shown that the present painting was prepared with a combination of oil and wax, a technique which Reynolds began to employ from the mid-1760s, and which provided him with a malleable but vulnerable picture surface and one he explored in

his attempts to capture the effects of old master painters.[12] Reynolds was famous for attempting to understand historic process by exploring the underpainting of old masters he acquired at auction. Samuel Redgrave recounted a contemporary anecdote of a pupil of Benjamin West: 'who possessed portraits by both Titian and Rubens which he said had belonged to Sir Joshua, and parts of which, to obtain wished-for secret, had been scraped or rubbed down to the panel, to lay bare the under-painting or dead colouring.'[13]

The early history of *Dionysius Areopagite*, once it left Reynolds's possession, is

unknown. The nineteenth-century cataloguers of Reynolds's *oeuvre*, Algernon Graves and William Vine Cronin, speculated that it may have been the work purchased at Reynolds's posthumous sale of 1796 by Joseph Farington, entitled 'An old man's head looking up'.[14] Martin Postle has suggested other possibilities.[15] By 1850, when it was first exhibited in public at the British Institution (no.55 'Dionysius the Areopagite'), the picture was owned by John Bentley, whose armorial bookplate is still pasted to the back of the canvas. Both John Bentley, whose seat was at Birch House, Farnworth, Lancashire, and his

Sir Joshua Reynolds
Count Ugolino and his children in the dungeon, 1770–3
Oil on canvas
20½ × 28⅜ inches · 520 × 720 mm
Knole, Kent
© National Trust Images / Brian Tremain

father, also John Bentley, purchased great eighteenth-century British pictures. As well as *Dionysius Areopagite*, Bentley's posthumous sale of 1886 included Joseph Wright of Derby's *Corinthian Maid* and his *Italian Landscape (San Cosimato)*, both now in the collection of the National Gallery of Art, Washington, versions of *Apollo and the Seasons* by Richard Wilson and a version of *The Cottage Door* by Gainsborough (possibly by Gainsborough Dupont), as well as works by William Dobson, Peter Lely, Thomas Lawrence, George Romney, and Samuel Scott.[16] Following Bentley's posthumous sale, the picture passed to the owner of West Bilney Hall, East Winch, Norfolk, where it was last recorded in 1905.

The rediscovery of this major work by Reynolds adds an important canvas to a crucial moment in the development of his art. Painted at the moment Reynolds transformed his practice from commercial portraiture to encompass history painting and from a private man of business to a public artist and President of the Royal Academy, the *Dionysius Areopogite* is a fascinating and emblematic painting. Conceived as a life study of Reynolds's favourite model, George White, it was published as an historical work which looked back to both Raphael and Rembrandt. As well as its historical significance, the *Dionysius Areopogite* is a profoundly moving and exquisitely painted celebration of Reynolds's powers at characterisation and fluency as a technician. As an addition to Reynolds's *oeuvre* its importance cannot be overstated and will accordingly form the subject of an article in *The Burlington Magazine* written by Dr Martin Postle.

NOTES

1 Martin Postle, *Sir Joshua Reynolds: the subject pictures*, Cambridge, 1995, pp.125–126. David Mannings and Martin Postle, *Sir Joshua Reynolds: A Complete Catalogue of his Paintings,* New Haven and London, 2000, no.2066, p.528 (as untraced).

2 For George White see Martin Postle, 'Patriarchs, prophets, and paviours: Reynolds's images of old age', *The Burlington Magazine*, 1988, vol.cxxx, pp.736–37 and Martin Postle, *Sir Joshua Reynolds: the subject pictures*, Cambridge, 1995, pp.121–160.

3 Martin Postle, *Sir Joshua Reynolds: the subject pictures*, Cambridge, 1995, p.125.

4 Martin Postle, *Sir Joshua Reynolds: the subject pictures*, Cambridge, 1995, pp.121–160.

5 For other artists who used White see: Martin Postle, 'Patriarchs, prophets, and paviours: Reynolds's images of old age', *The Burlington Magazine*, 1988, vol.cxxx, pp.739–740.

6 1818, 1, pp.278–283.

7 Martin Postle, *Sir Joshua Reynolds: the subject pictures*, Cambridge, 1995, pp.138–140.

8 J. Richardson, 1715, pp.93–4.

9 For Reynolds's collection see Francis Broun, 'Sir Joshua Reynolds's collection of paintings', unpublished PhD thesis, Princeton University, 1987, pp.182–9.

10 Ed. Nancy Petersen, *Timken Museum of Art*, 1996, pp.90–93.

11 Ed. Robert Wark, *Sir Joshua Reynolds: Discourses on Art*, New Haven and London, 1975, p.223.

12 For Reynolds's use of wax see Helene Dubois, "Use a little wax with your colours, but don't tell anybody". Reynolds's Painting Experiments with wax and his sources, *Hamilton Kerr Institute Bulletin*, Number 3, 2000, pp.97–106.

13 M. Kirby Talley, 'All Goof Pictures Crack', Sir Joshua Reynolds's practice and studio', in ed. Nicholas Penny, *Reynolds*, exh.cat. London (Royal Academy of Arts), 1985, pp.56–57.

14 Sold Greenwood's, 15 April 1796 (56) for £21. See Algernon Graves and William Vine Cronin, *A History of the Works of Sir Joshua Reynolds*, 4 vols., London 1899–1901, vol.3, pp.149–50.

15 Postle in Mannings and Postle, *op. cit.*, vol.1, p.528.

16 The Collection of John Bentley, Esq., deceased, late of Birch House, Lancashire, and Portland Place, Christie's 15 May 1886.

DANIEL GARDNER *c.1750–1805*

The Hon. Mary Shuttleworth, née Cockburn (d.1777) and her sister *Anna Maria, 9th Baroness Forrester (d.1808)*

Pastel and gouache on paper laid on canvas, on their original backboards
Oval 20 × 17 inches · 530 × 455 mm
Executed in 1776

This striking, recently rediscovered pair of portraits of Anna Maria, 9th Baroness Forrester and her sister, the Hon Mary Shuttleworth, show Daniel Gardner at the height of his powers as a portraitist. The sitters were the daughters of the Hon. Caroline Baillie, Baroness Forrester and her husband Capt. George Cockburn RN of Ormiston, East Lothian who was Comptroller of the Navy from 1756 until 1770. The portraits seem likely to have been executed in 1776, the year Mary Cockburn married the Rev. Charles Shuttleworth of Aston in Derbyshire. Her elder sister, Anna Maria, became the 9th Baroness Forrester on the death of their mother, but died without issue.

Gardner's portraiture occupies an unusual position within the history of British painting during the eighteenth century. By the late 1770s, Gardner was one of the most successful and prolific painters in London having created a hugely popular portrait formula; reproducing in pastel on a reduced-scale the fashionable poses and conceits of full-sized works by Sir Joshua Reynolds and George Romney. Conversely, unlike the masters he imitated, Gardner's success was achieved without the use of London's exhibiting societies: he showed only one picture at the Royal Academy and never submitted a work to the Society of Artists. As a result Gardner has received comparatively little scholarly attention, although the range, importance and number of his sitters suggests that he was a significant member of the wider artistic community and his beautifully executed and engaging portraits are a fascinating testament to the success and adaptability of 'Grand Manner' portraiture.[1] All these elements are

visible in the present hugely accomplished and finely handled portraits.

Gardner was born in Kendal in Cumbria and after leaving school worked with George Romney. Romney himself had left Kendal for London in 1762, and Gardner followed in either 1767 or 1768, living initially at 11 Cockspur Street, very close to the Royal Academy Schools in Pall Mall which he joined in 1770.[2] On leaving the schools, Gardner joined Joshua Reynolds's studio as an assistant in exchange for further tuition. Gardner was therefore working for Reynolds at the moment he was experimenting with his grandest and most impressive exhibition portraits. Shortly after establishing his own practice, Gardner began to produce works in pastel which closely followed the fashions established by his former master, simply replicating poses and compositions on a more domestic scale. The present portraits perfectly illustrate Gardner's working method. *Mary Shuttleworth* is shown with her hand resting on her chin, dressed in loose classical costume, in a pose which is modelled on Reynolds's full-length portrait of *Mary, Duchess of Ancaster* now at Houghton Hall, Norfolk. The addition of an urn and still life of flowers adds to the decorative quality of the composition.

Gardner developed a novel technique using pastel to approximate the appearance of oil. By combining pure pastel with a liquid vehicle he was able to create a range of textures, from the soft rendering of features and hair, to the more broadly handled landscape of *Lady Forrester*.[3] In the present work the areas of greatest opacity, such as the costumes, are created using

Gardner's distinctive technique. The domestic scale of Gardner's works, their charm and sweetness meant he was frequently commissioned to paint family groups and children. The present pair are an extremely fine example of Gardner's technique and manner, perfectly illustrating why he was such a successful artist. It was Gardner's clever distillation of Reynolds and Romney's style into a domestic scale which made him extremely popular with American collectors of the early twentieth century.

John Dixon, after Sir Joshua Reynolds
Her Grace Mary, Duchess of Ancaster and Kesteven,
1765–71
Mezzotint · 24⅜ × 15 inches · 620 × 380 mm
© The Trustees of the British Museum

NOTES

1 Gardner was the subject of an exhibition at Kenwood House: Helen Kapp, *Daniel Gardner 1750 – 1805*, exh.cat. London (Kenwoood House), 1972 and a book: George Williamson, *Daniel Gardner*, London, 1921. But comparatively little has been written about him subsequently and he is omitted from standard accounts of eighteenth-century British art.

2 Helen Kapp, *Daniel Gardner 1750 – 1805*, exh.cat. London (Kenwoood House), 1972, unpaginated introduction.

3 Neil Jeffares, *Dictionary of Pastellists before 1800*, London, 2006, p.191.

JOHN ROBERT COZENS 1752–1797

Hannibal Showing to his Army the Fertile Plains of Italy

Pencil and grey wash
10¼ inches · 260 mm diameter
Drawn in 1776

COLLECTIONS
Sotheby's, 17th May 1933, lot 11;
Walker's Galleries, London;
The Fine Arts Society, London;
Joseph and Deborah Goldyne;
Private collection, USA, to 2013.

LITERATURE
A.P. Oppé, *Alexander and John Robert Cozens*,
London, 1952, pp.125–127;
Jospeh R. Goldyne, *J.M.W. Turner: Works on
Paper from American Collections*, 1975, p.182;
Andrew Wilton, *The Art of Alexander and John
Robert Cozens*, exh.cat., New Haven (Yale
Center for British Art), 1980, p.9;
Kim Sloan, *Alexander and John Robert Cozens:
The Poetry of Landscape*, New Haven and
London, 1986, fig.120, pp.101, 103–105, 109–112.

EXHIBITED
London, Walker's Galleries, 1934, no.22;
London, The Fine Art Society, 1968, no.109;
Berkeley, University Art Museum, J.M.W
*Turner: Works on Paper from American
Collections*, 1975, no.62.

This watercolour is part of a small group made by John Robert Cozens in the same format in about 1776 which depict historical scenes. The dramatic, concentrated roundels demonstrate Cozens's early absorption of his father, Alexander's innovative pictorial techniques, but in their breadth of handling and communication of intense atmosphere point towards the sublimity of his mature works. The subject of this roundel in particular is of great historical importance. Illustrating a passage from Livy, showing Hannibal and his men viewing the Po valley beyond the foothills of the Alps, a scene no other artist had chosen as the subject of a history painting during the eighteenth century. Perhaps more importantly it was a subject which Cozens would treat again in his only recorded oil painting, exhibited at the Royal Academy in 1776. As the nineteenth-century painter and art writer C.R. Leslie noted:

John Robert Cozens exhibited only one oil at the Royal Academy during his lifetime, a picture entitled A Landscape with Hannibal in His March Over the Alps, Showing to His Army Fertile Plains of Italy. This I have heard was an oil picture so fine that Turner spoke it as a work from which he learned more than anything he had then seen.[1]

Cozens's great oil painting of *Hannibal in His March Over the Alps* has been missing since 1876 making the present wash roundel a crucial piece of evidence in understanding the lost work.[2] *Hannibal Showing to his Army the Fertile Plains of Italy* is also one of the most compelling early essays by Cozens executed before he took his transformative trip to Italy later the same year with Richard Payne Knight.

John Robert Cozens
Satan Summoning his Legions, c.1776
Watercolour · 11⅜ × 13⅛ inches · 288 × 334 mm
© Tate, London 2014, purchased as part of the Oppé
Collection with assistance from the National Lottery
through the Heritage Lottery Fund 1996

Alexander Cozens
*A Sublime Composition: a Lake in a
Mountain Landscape*
Brown washes over pencil with gum arabic
14¾ × 10¾ inches · 375 × 275 mm
Musée du Louvre (formerly with Lowell Libson Ltd)

The composition of the present work, like the other roundels from the same sequence, show John Robert Cozens experimenting with the kind of fantastic rock formations most closely associated with the work of his father, Alexander Cozens.[3] Indeed it has been suggested that these early roundels actually evolved from blots. Alexander Cozens had developed a method of compositional invention which was reliant on accidental or random mark making – known as blot drawings – to form the basis for more finished landscape sheets. The present drawing, which shows Hannibal and his men standing on a jagged escarpment with a subtly receding landscape in the background, anticipates the kind of Alpine view Cozens would become famous for depicting after his Continental tour, pointing to an early technical sophistication. It has not previously been noted but in one of the other roundels in this group, the *Fleet at Anchor in a Rocky Cove* (possibly *Ulysses's Fleet in the Bay of* Laestrigonia) now in the Sarah Campbell Blaffer Foundation, Houston, Cozens uses scratching out to suggest the spray on the rocks, a technique he would pioneer in his later Alpine views.[4]

The precise context of the existing roundels is unclear. The first four appeared on the market in 1933, the fifth at auction in 1951 having descended from Cozens's illegitimate daughter; whilst two of them seem to depict Miltonic subject-matter and two Homeric subjects, the fifth is *Hannibal in His March Over the Alps* from Livy. Given their format, they may well have been designed as book illustrations and Oppé even suggested that they may be associated with an uncompleted project initiated by William Beckford.[5] This imaginative watercolour stands as important evidence for Cozens's pre-Italian work, his technical breadth and compositional innovation. The image also preserves Cozens's most innovative subject matter and provides significant evidence for his lost oil, a work which had tremendous impact on Turner and the conception of sublime landscape in the Romantic era.

NOTES

1   C.R. Lewis, *A Handbook for Young Painters*, London, 1855, p.263.
2   Kim Sloan, *Alexander and John Robert Cozens / The Poetry of Landscape*, New Haven and London, 1986, pp.103–105.
3   Andrew Wilton, *The Art of Alexander and John Robert Cozens*, exh.cat., New Haven (Yale Center for British Art), 1980, p.9.
4   Martin Butlin, *Aspects of British Painting 1550–1800: From the Collection of the Sarah Campbell Blaffer Foundation*, Houston, 1988,
5   A.P.Oppé *Alexander and John Robert Cozens*, London, 1952p.126–127.

JOHN ROBERT COZENS 1752–1799

An Alpine Landscape, near Grindelwald, Switzerland

Pen and brown ink and brown and grey blue
wash, on two joined sheets
14½ × 18½ inches · 368 × 470 mm
Executed in 1776

COLLECTIONS
John Spink, London;
Private collection, USA, 2014.

This drawing was made on John Robert
Cozens's first, hugely influential Continental
trip. Travelling in the company of the great
collector and connoisseur Richard Payne
Knight, Cozens set out for Italy in August
1776, first undertaking a short Alpine tour.
It was in the monumental landscape of the
Alps that Cozens saw at first hand the ideas
of the sublime in nature which he had learnt
from his artist father, Alexander Cozens
and other theorists, such as Edmund Burke.
The watercolours Cozens produced over
his two months in France and Switzerland
are regarded as some of the most compelling of the eighteenth century and as Kim
Sloan has noted, in them: 'Cozens had
finally lifted watercolour painting out of the
topographical recording of nature, to a new
level where it was capable of fulfilling the
serious intentions of art as oil painting.'[1]

Cozens and Payne Knight followed a typical round trip from Geneva which included
visiting Bonneville, Cluse, Sallanches, Mont
Blanc, Chamonix and Martigny before head-
ing through Interlaken and Grindelwald. In
a contemporary guidebook, the area was
described in the following terms:
*The overhanging rocks of a prodigious height,
and torrents pouring down in sheets from their
very summits, are such wonders of Nature, as it
is impossible to look upon without a mixture of
astonishment and awe.*[2]

This combination of 'astonishment and
awe' were precisely the feelings Cozens
captured in the drawings he made for Payne
Knight. The present unusual view was made
close to Grindelwald, possibly in the valley
of Ober-Hasli close to the Reichenbach falls.

Drawn in the autumn of 1776 this bold
and striking sheet depicts the Reichenbach
stream running close to Grindelwald with
the Wetterhorn in the distance. Unlike

John Robert Cozens
*Near the valley of Ober-hasli, view on the
Reichenbach, 1776*
Pen and grey ink and grey wash, touched with watercolour
14⅛ × 9⅛ inches · 357 × 231 mm
© The Trustees of the British Museum

Cozens's earliest Alpine views, it does not depict a sweeping valley floor, the expansive views of his Savoyard scenes have been cropped, to focus on the stark grandeur of the mountains themselves. As Kim Sloan has noted, Cozens's views of the Reichenbach are: 'realized by the elimination of traditional compositional tools. Distance and horizons are no longer represented and the viewer is faced with a sheer wall of rock that threatens to enclose him by surrounding or reaching over him, and blocking out even the sky.'[3]

Cozens has taken evident delight in the towering rock formations, placing the escarpment on the left almost at the top of the composition, encroaching far into the space generally reserved for the sky. The view shows a debt to Alexander Cozens's theory of composition which demanded that masses should alternate on either side, thus the peaks on the left are shown as lower, with a wedge shaped valley in between.[4] The economic, almost monochrome palette adds to the drama of the scene, giving the masses of the

mountains covered in spiky, skeletal trees an almost menacing quality. Indeed the drawing is close to one prepared by Alexander Cozens in his *Various Species of Composition of Landscapes in Nature* which entitled: 'Tops of Hills or Mountains'.

Cozens was deeply affected by the sublime nature of the Alpine landscape, but he mediated his response through the compositional theories of his father and contemporary literary and poetic associations. Recent work has shown that very few watercolours were made 'on the spot' by British artists travelling on the Continent and from the visual evidence, Cozens's Payne Knight Alpine watercolours were long thought to be based on a series of drawings assumed no longer to survive.[5] The present highly energized drawing and its, rough, spontaneous finish suggest that the present sheet may well be one of the drawings Cozens made on the spot.

Regardless of its status, the present drawing is a particularly important example

from Cozens's first great series of landscape watercolours; a visual essay on responses to the sublime in nature. Cozens's *Alpine Landscape near Grindelwald* and other sheets from this trip, had an enormous impact upon the next generation of landscape artists in Britain, including J.M.W. Turner and Thomas Girtin.

NOTES

1   Kim Sloan, *Alexander and John Robert Cozens: The Poetry of* Landscape, New Haven and London, 1986, p.125.

2   M. Bourrit, trans. C. Davy, *A Relation of a Journey to the Glaciers in the Dutchy of* Savoy, Norwich, 1776, p.2.

3   Kim Sloan, *Alexander and John Robert Cozens: The Poetry of* Landscape, New Haven and London, 1986, p.120.

4   Kim Sloan, *Alexander and John Robert Cozens: The Poetry of* Landscape, New Haven and London, 1986, pp.36–62.

5   For a discussion of the Alpine material see: Kim Sloan, *Alexander and John Robert Cozens: The Poetry of Landscape*, New Haven and London, 1986,pp.115–116.

above: John Robert Cozens *First view of the Reichenbach between Grindelwald and the Vale of Ober-Hasli, 1776*
Brush drawing in grey wash with watercolour · 9⅛ × 13⅞ inches · 231 × 353 mm
© The Trustees of the British Museum

left: John Robert Cozens *Second view on the Reichenbach near Meiringen in the valley of Ober-Hasli, 1776*
Pen and grey ink and grey wash, touched with watercolour n· 9⅛ × 14 inches · 233 × 355 mm
© The Trustees of the British Museum

THOMAS JONES 1742–1803
Montmélian in Savoy

Oil on paper laid down on canvas
13½ × 21¾ inches · 343 × 552 mm
Signed and inscribed: 'MONT MELIAN / in
Savoy / T. JONES no.XVIII' (lower right)
Painted in 1776

COLLECTIONS
Thomas Jones,
Anna Maria Thomas, daughter of the above;
Jane Evan-Thomas, by descent;
Private collection, by gift from the above,
1986;
Private collection, USA, 2014.

LITERATURE
Paul. Oppé (ed.), 'Memoirs of Thomas
Jones, Penkerrig, Radnorshire, 1803', *The
Walpole Society*, vol.XXXII, 1946–8, p.44;
Ann Sumner and Greg Smith (ed.), *Thomas
Jones (1742–1803): An Artist Rediscovered*, exh.
cat., London, 2003, p.177, repr.

EXHIBITED
Cardiff, National Museum of Wales,
Manchester, Whitworth Art Gallery
and London, National Gallery, *Thomas
Jones (1742–1803): An Artist Rediscovered*,
2003–4, no.67.

Thomas Jones
Near Chambéry in the Savoy, 1776
Oil on paper laid on canvas
13 × 21⅜ inches · 328 × 542 mm
Signed, inscribed and dated: *near CHAMBERI in Savoy.*
T JONES NoXVI
Private collection (formerly with Lowell Libson Ltd)

This boldly handled painting dates from
Thomas Jones's important European Grand
Tour, when he executed a series of celebrated
oil sketches of landscapes and buildings.
Successful during his own lifetime, but largely
forgotten after his death, Jones has received
a great deal of attention in recent years as a
result of these powerful *plein air* studies. The
present view, which is unusually ambitious
and expansive in its scope, was painted at
the beginning of Jones's tour, as he travelled
through France to Rome. Carefully inscribed
'Mont Melian/in Savoy/ T. Jones No.XVIII'
it formed part of a sequence of views which
remained in Jones's family and passed to his
daughters.[1] Following Thomas Jones's death
in 1803, his pictures were inherited by his two
daughters, Anna Maria and Elizabeth. The
present picture descended to Jones's elder
daughter, Anna Maria who married Thomas
Thomas Esq. of Llanbradach, Glamorgan.

In the autumn of 1770 Thomas Jones
recorded in his *Memoirs* a trip to Gadbridge,
Buckinghamshire, the home of his cousin
Rice James: 'made a number of Sketches from
the little picturesque Bits round about, as far
as St Alban's, and painted in Oil some Studies
of Trees &c after nature.'[2] This is the most
substantive reference in Jones's own writing
to his technique of producing studies from
nature on primed paper small enough to fit
into the lid of a painting-box. This innovative
technique became an important feature of
his Continental work. Indeed, whilst in Italy,
Jones met a number of French, German and
Scandinavian artists who were beginning to
make use of the on-the-spot oil study, including Pierre-Henri de Valenciennes.

On Saturday 2 November 1776 Thomas
Jones recorded in his journal his journey in
Savoy from Chambéry through Montmélian

to a hostelry at Planaise, noting:
*Some effects of Light & Shade from broken Clouds
& rugged Mountains were wonderfully fine, made
a Sketch of Montmelian from hence*[4]

The present atmospheric view of the town
of Montmélian seems likely to have been the
result. Jones frequently made *plein air* drawings which he subsequently worked-up in oil.
The present painting was begun on paper
– probably as a drawing – then painted over
in oil and later laid down on canvas; this small
painting can therefore be identified as the
'Sketch of *Montmelian*' made from Planaise
recorded in Jones's diary. The expansive
view shows the landscape of Savoy, where
a field is being ploughed in the foreground,
beyond is the town of Montmélian with the
distinctive arches of the Pont de l'Isère in
the foreground.

In its combination of subject matter, technique and atmosphere, this work is an impressive example of Jones's rare Continental oil
sketches. As such it is not only a significant
work by a crucial British painter, but a work
which has a wider European significance,
offering a valuable precedent for the count-
less French, German and British painters who
would produce oil, landscape studies *en plein
air* in Italy after 1800.

NOTES

1   See eds. Ann Sumner and Greg Smith, *Thomas
    Jones (1742–1803): An Artist Rediscovered,* exh.
    cat., Cardiff (National Museum & Gallery of
    Wales), 2003, p.176 for another oil landscape in
    this sequence.
2   Ed. P. Oppé, 'Memoirs of Thomas Jones,
    Penkerrig, Radnorshire, 1803', *The Walpole
    Society*, vol.32, 1946–8, p.22.
3   Ed. Paul Oppé, Paul. Oppé, 'Memoirs of
    Thomas Jones, Penkerrig, Radnorshire, 1803',
    The Walpole Society, 32, 1946–8, p.44.

GEORGE ROMNEY 1734–1802

Study for 'The Leveson-Gower Children'

Pen and brown ink and brown wash
9⅜ × 9½ inches · 238 × 241 mm
Drawn 1776

COLLECTIONS
The artist;
Elizabeth Romney, by descent, to 1894;
Romney sale, Christie's, 24–25 May 1894
(part of an unidentified lot);
Lawrence Romney, purchased at the
above sale;
J.S. Maas & Co.;
Robert Harford, by 1978;
Thos. Agnew & Sons, 2002;
Private collection, 2014.

LITERATURE
Alex Kidson, *George Romney 1734–1802*,
exh.cat., London, 2002, pp.115–17.

EXHIBITED
London, Burlington Fine Arts Club, *Pictures,
Decorative Arts and other Works of Art*, 1916,
no.85;
Kendal, Abbot Hall Art Gallery, on long
term loan, 1978 to 1999;
Kendal, Abbot Hall Art Gallery, *George
Romney 1734–1802*, 1984, no.3;
Liverpool, Walker Art Gallery, *George Romney
1734–1802*, 2002, no.57;
London, National Portrait Gallery, *George
Romney 1734–1802*, 2002, no.57;
London, Agnew's, *Romney Drawings*, 2002,
no.1.

This is the largest and most impressive preparatory drawing for Romney's famous portrait of the *Gower Children* now in Abbot Hall Art Gallery, Kendal. Romney was a bold and incisive draughtsman who made numerous rich brown ink studies, principally for historical compositions; by contrast, comparatively few studies linked directly to his portraits survive. The existence of a group of studies for the *Gower Children* underscores its importance to Romney. The sitters were the five youngest of the eight children of Granville, 2nd Earl Gower who, at the time the portrait was commissioned, was President of the Council in Lord North's government and one of the best-connected and most influential people in England. The present drawing which is a large scale treatment of the composition in its final form perfectly distils Romney's conceit: the younger children dancing whilst their elder sister, in the guise of a Bacchante plays the tambourine. The bold and dramatic study underlines both the artistic confidence and classical grandeur Romney gained during his trip to Italy between 1773 and 1775.

The commission from Granville, 2nd Earl Gower to paint five of his children came shortly after Romney's Continental tour.[1] The initial idea, as represented by the present drawing, seems to have been to paint Lady Anne, the figure on the right of the composition playing the tambourine, who was the youngest of Gower's first four children by his second wife Lady Louisa Egerton and who married the Rev. Edward Vernon Harcourt, later Archbishop of York, with three of her younger half-siblings by Gower's third wife, Lady Susanna Stewart: at the left Lady Georgina, who became Countess of St Germans following her marriage to the Hon. William Eliot; at the right Lady Charlotte Sophia, later Duchess of Beaufort and in the centre Lady Susanna, later Countess of Harrowby. Romney added a fifth child to the finished portrait,

George Romney
*The Gower Family:
The Children of Granville,
2nd Earl Gower*
*c.*1776–77
Oil on canvas
80 × 92½ inches
2030 × 2350 mm
Abbott Hall, Kendal (formerly
with Leger Galleries)

Gower's son: Lord Granville, later created Viscount Granville and Earl Granville. In Italy Romney had produced a large number of studies of classical antiquities and old master paintings.

The commission from Gower offered Romney the opportunity to explore a complex multi-figural group, putting into practice the kind of ambitious classical quotations that Reynolds was currently exploiting. In 1773 Reynolds had completed the remarkable group portrait of the *Montgomery Sisters*, now in the Tate Gallery, London, which showed them adorning a herm of the Roman god Hymen; the composition used a garland to link the three figures who were shown in classical costume dancing at the foot of a Roman sculpture.[2] Scholars have long pointed to a similar sources for the two compositions: the works of Nicolas Poussin. Whilst the *Montgomery Sisters* is based, in part, on a *Bacchanal* now in the Musée des Beaux-Arts, the *Gower Children* has always been associated with Poussin's *Dance to the Music of Time*, now in

the Wallace Collection, London. It seems more likely that Romney was looking to an antique source in the form of the Borghese Dancers, a Roman relief, then in Palazzo Borghese in Rome. Romney would have seen the relief of interlocking, dancing maidens and would also have known Guido Reni's *Aurora*, the fresco on the ceiling of the Casino at Palazzo Pallavicini-Rospigliosi, which also relied upon the Borghese Dancers.

In the present drawing, Romney has structured a composition which uses the idea of interlocking female figures animated in dance for a portrait study: the three youngest daughters are carefully articulated so that their faces are visible. In the *Gower Children* Romney had a patron and commission which offered the perfect opportunity to demonstrate the vocabulary of quotations from classical antiquity and old master paintings he had acquired in Italy; the 'materials of genius' praised by Reynolds in his *Discourses*. Conscious of the prevailing fashion for semi-historicised portraits

in, what Reynolds termed, the 'great style', Romney formulated an erudite formula which would appeal to his aristocratic patron and his peers; Reynolds noted in his last *Discourse* that such portraits were 'artificial in the highest degree, it presupposes in the spectator, a cultivated and prepared artificial state of mind.'[3] The bold, almost abstract, forms and incisive draughtsmanship of the present drawing demonstrate Romney's ability to conceive and formulate a powerful composition on the page. Executed with rich brown ink, this sheet is one of the boldest and most spectacular of Romney's surviving portrait drawings.

NOTES

1 Alex Kidson, *George Romney 1734–1802*, exh.cat., London (National Portrait Gallery), London, 2002, pp.114–117.
2 Ed. Nicholas Penny, *Reynolds*, exh.cat., London (Royal Academy of Arts), 1986, no.90, pp.262–263.
3 Ed. Robert Wark, *The Discourses of Joshua Reynolds*, New Haven and London, 1975, p.277.

Giovanni Domenico Campiglia
The Borghese Dancers
Black chalk · 10¾ × 19⅞ inches · 274 × 505 mm
© The Trustees of the British Museum

W. Holl, After Sir Joshua Reynolds
Portraits of three ladies adorning the altar of Hymen, the daughters of William Montgomery
Stipple engraving, 1836
10¾ × 8½ inches · 272 × 215 mm
© The Trustees of the British Museum

JOHN SINGLETON COPLEY RA 1738–1815

Sir William Pepperrell and Family

Black, white and red chalk
17 × 21½ inches · 430 × 545 mm
Drawn in 1778

COLLECTIONS
John Singleton Copley RA, the artist;
John Singleton Copley, 1st Baron Lyndhurst
(1772–1863), son of the above;
The Hon. Georgiana Susan Copley, daughter
of the above, m.1863 Sir Charles Du Cane;
Charles Henry Copley Du Cane (1864–1938),
son of the above;
Peter Du Cane (1901–1984), son of the above;
and by descent, 2014.

LITERATURE
Jules D. Prown, *John Singleton Copley: England
1774–1815*, 1966, p.429, repr. plate 357.

This important drawing was made by John Singleton Copley in preparation for what was the most ambitious and prestigious of the commissions which he received on his arrival in London following his Grand Tour in 1775. Depicting the family of Sir William Pepperrell, the most prominent American Loyalist exiled in London during the American Revolutionary War, the drawing provides important insight into Copley's working method and the complex visual and intellectual process undertaken by the first generation of Royal Academicians in preparing 'Grand Manner' portraits for exhibition in London. The highly sophisticated drawing, rendered in black, white and red chalk, demonstrates in both the use of Italianate poses and the careful articulation of the composition Copley's newly found sophistication, following his period of Continental study. The sheet is also historically significant in depicting the family of a leading Loyalist by a Loyalist painter at the height of hostilities in America; presenting an image of prosperity and domestic contentment at a moment of profound personal and public turmoil.

John Singleton Copley was born in Boston in 1738 and despite the lack of access to European old masters or a European artist's studio, he forged a successful portrait practice in Boston. By copying the English engravings available in Boston he evolved a highly distinctive style by the late 1750s, which was highly descriptive and marked by meticulous detail, crisp lines and edges, strong colour, and dramatic tonal contrasts. From the early 1760s Copley was urged to visit Europe by correspondents in London, including the American painter Benjamin West and President of the Royal Academy,

Sir Joshua Reynolds, who observed: 'your Manner and Taste were corrupted or fixed by working in your little way at Boston.'[1]

In 1767 Copley dispatched a portrait for exhibition at the Royal Academy, the Young Lady with a Bird and Dog now in the Toledo Museum of Art, Ohio, but to English academic eyes Copley's work fell short of the prevailing fashionable manner. Citing first the overall detailing and the opacity and brightness of colour, West wrote to him that: 'Each Part being…Equell in Strength of Coulering and finishing, Each Making too much a Picture of its silf, without that Due Subordanation to the Principle parts, viz they head and hands.'[2] He repeated the admonition to come 'home' to London 'before it may be too late for much Improvement.'[3] It was not until the Boston Tea Party in December 1773 that Copley took the decision to move his family to Europe. Despite being friends with – and having painted – prominent Whig Patriots such as Samuel Adams and Paul Revere, Copley was a Loyalist. More immediately Copley's father-in-law, Richard Clarke, who had the exclusive contract from the East India Company to import tea, was subject to ferocious Whig attacks. It was from Clarke's own ship that a group of activists disguised as Mohawks dumped 342 casks of tea into Boston harbour in December 1773 (the so-called Boston Tea Party). As a result in June 1774 Copley and the extended Clarke family set out for Britain.

Shortly after arriving in London, Copley undertook a short Grand Tour to the Continent with the older English artist George Carter, where exposure to Italian old master paintings and great antiquities prompted a wholesale change in his

John Singleton Copley
Sir William Pepperrell and his Family, 1778
Oil on canvas · 90 × 108 inches · 2286 × 2743 mm
North Carolina Museum of Art, Raleigh, Purchased with funds
from the State of North Carolina

approach to painting. Copley began in Italy his first independent historical work, the *Ascension* (Museum of Fine Arts, Boston) made in conscious emulation of Raphael, and most complex group portrait to date: *Mr and Mrs Ralph Izard* (Museum of Fine Arts, Boston). But most importantly, Copley's exposure to Italian old master's resulted in a softening of his approach and adoption of a more painterly technique. On returning to London in 1766 he moved to a house in Leicester Fields before beginning his ambitious self-portrait: *The Copley Family* (National Gallery of Art, Washington). This was followed by an even bolder group composition, the magnificent portrait of *Sir William Pepperell and Family* which was shown at the Royal Academy in 1778.

The political situation which prompted Copley's decision to leave America also dislodged the Loyalist William Sparhawk Pepperrell. Pepperrell's grandfather, William Pepperrell II, had been knighted by George II in 1746 for his role in capturing the French garrison at Louisburg in Cape Breton, the first native colonial to receive the honour.[4] Pepperrell inherited his grandfather's vast fortune, land and position in New England, being chosen as a member of the Governor's Council (although a recommendation to succeed Thomas Hutchinson as Governor of Massachusetts in 1773 was not acted upon).[5] Pepperrell married Elizabeth Royall, the daughter of one of the most prominent and wealthy merchant families in New England, who had sat to Copley as a child (Museum of Fine Art, Boston). In 1774 the baronetcy was revived in his favour, but shortly afterwards the York County Congress (near Kittery, Maine, the home of the Pepperrell family) passed a resolution declaring that Sir

William, a Loyalist, should be 'detested by all good men,' and that tenants who lived off his land should break all ties with his family.[6] Before Pepperrell finally decided to flee to Britain, Elizabeth (known as Betsy) succumbed to dysentery and died in Boston.

Pepperrell therefore arrived in London an exiled widower, with a young family denied an income from his very considerable American lands and property and facing an uncertain future. His decision to commission Copley to paint a conversation piece of his entire family, including his deceased wife, requires some explanation. Pepperrell, as the only American baronet, was an important figurehead for Loyalists in London and was undoubtedly determined to project an image

of domestic contentment and continuity as well as underlining to a London audience the extent of his personal losses in supporting the Loyalist cause. Pepperrell's surviving correspondence shows that, as chairman of the Loyalist Association, he worked hard to assist other Loyalists (both in Britain and America) in obtaining compensation and pensions from the British Treasury, whilst also communicating regularly with members of the British government about the situation in America. Copley and Pepperrell knew each other in London, both were active members of the New England Club moving in similar Loyalist circles.[7] As a result of the prestige of the sitter, the fact that this was the first major portrait commission Copley

had received after his return to London from Italy and that it was undoubtedly destined for the very public walls of the Royal Academy Exhibition, he spent a great deal of time in preparing the composition executing five drawn studies.

The present sheet is the largest and most impressive of the surviving drawings, but at least three figure studies survive: one depicting Pepperrell's four children seated around Elizabeth Pepperrell (Museum of Fine Arts, Boston); a study of the youngest child, William, in his mother's arms (Museum of Fine Arts, Boston) and a squared study of Sir William standing, which is drawn on the back of a study for the *Ascension* presumably made in Italy (Victoria and Albert Museum, London).[8] They demonstrate the way Copley played with the relationship of the central figures, introducing new conceits and combinations and indicate a visual restlessness which is evidence of his recent trip to Italy and his exposure to a wealth of new visual stimuli.

The present sheet shows Sir William standing on the left, one arm around his eldest daughter Elizabeth, the other holding a piece of drapery over his wife's head. The action, mirrored by his youngest child, William, forms a make-shift canopy over his dead wife. On the far right of the composition, Mary and Harriot Pepperrell are depicted playing skittles. One of the most remarkable features of the present sheet is the inclusion, on the far right, of a black servant, which Copley eliminates in another (apparently later) compositional study and the final painting.[9] This may well have been a servant in the Pepperrell's household; it is known that they travelled from Boston with a Quaker nanny and undoubtedly other

servants.[10] Pepperrell had a large estate in Surinam which provided income whilst he was in London (until the Dutch entered the American Revolutionary War in December 1780); it seems likely that the turbaned servant was an actual member of the household, rather than a device of Copley's invention. Jules Prown has persuasively suggested that Copley used his own family to facilitate the composition of the design of this complex group portrait and that the present sheet depicts members of Copley's family instead of the Pepperrells: he posits that Copley's wife, Sukey, took the place of the deceased Elizabeth Pepperrell and Copley's stepbrother, Henry Pelham, the place of Sir William.[11] Certainly the physiognomy of Elizabeth Pepperrell resembles Mrs Copley from the *Copley Family* (National Gallery of Art, Washington) and the features of Sir William are markedly different from the finished portrait.

As such the drawing gives a good sense of Copley's working method, differing greatly from the finished painting (North Carolina Museum of Art, Raleigh) and demonstrating his determination to achieve a composition which was both unified and visually arresting. Although the present drawing is his earliest full-scale study it is the boldest in conception and the most highly and carefully finished. Playing with light and shade, Copley introduces limited colour into the arm of Sir William to articulate it from the bold area of shade behind Elizabeth Pepperrell, the unusual gesture of the drapery held between father and son, is suggestive of both the informality of family life and Copley's recent Continental trip. Throughout the evolution of the composition, Copley conceived of the *Pepperrell*

John Singleton Copley
Mother and two children (study for The Pepperrell Family), 1777–8
Black and white chalk on pinkish buff paper
17¼ × 13¼ inches · 438 × 337 mm

Museum of Fine Arts, Boston, The M. and M. Karolik Collection of Eighteenth-Century American Arts, 39.272

John Singleton Copley
Mary and Eizabeth Royall, c.1758
Oil on canvas
57⅜ × 48⅛ inches · 1457 × 1222 cm
Museum of Fine Arts, Boston
Julia Knight Fox Fund, 25.49

Family in terms of a Renaissance altarpiece, posing Elizabeth Pepperrell and her only son as a Madonna and Child. In Parma in 1775 Copley had copied Correggio's great altarpiece known as *Il Giorno* and the impact of the central group – the Virgin with an animated Christ child flanked by male and female saints – certainly informed Copley's ideas for arranging the group.[12] Whilst he eschewed direct quotation, Copley followed Reynolds's demands, as articulated in the *Discourses*, of making 'slight sketches of the machinery and general management' of an admired painting which could then inform a new composition.[13]

On his return from the Continent Copley was focused on establishing himself within the competitive London art market and would have been conscious that such an impressive commission would have been exhibited publicly at the annual exhibition of the Royal Academy. Whilst the picture garnered some critical reaction in 1778, it was Copley's novel historical composition, *Watson and the Shark*, which was exhibited the same year, which was more noticed. Copley's composition also had to compete with contemporary works, such as Joshua Reynolds's *Marlborough Family* (Blenheim Palace, Oxfordshire) and despite lacking the dynamism found in his initial drawing, the canvas won a degree of praise.

This striking drawing, which remained with Copley's descendants until 2014, is a remarkable testament to Copley's ambition at a critical moment in his career. Perhaps more significantly, this sheet distils an extraordinary moment in the story of the American Revolutionary Wars. At the point it was completed, Pepperrell, the most prominent Loyalist in exile, still had hopes of

a peaceful resolution of the Revolutionary Wars and of returning to an America under British rule. Pepperrell's choice of Copley, the leading Loyalist painter in London, underlines the fact that this striking family group must be read as a political statement as much as a society portrait.

NOTES

1 Eds. C. F. Adams, G. Jones and W. Ford, 'Letters and Papers of John Singleton Copley and Henry Pelham,' 1739–1776, *The Massachusetts Historical Society*, vol.71, 1914, p.44.

2 Eds. C. F. Adams, G. Jones and W. Ford, 'Letters and Papers of John Singleton Copley and Henry Pelham,' 1739–1776, *The Massachusetts Historical Society*, vol.71, 1914, pp.56–7.

3 Eds. C. F. Adams, G. Jones and W. Ford, 'Letters and Papers of John Singleton Copley and Henry Pelham,' 1739–1776, *The Massachusetts Historical Society*, vol.71, 1914, p.60.

4 See Virginia Browne-Wilkinson, *Pepperrell Posterity*, Florence, 1982.

5 Neil Rolde, *Sir William Pepperrell of Colonial New England*, 1982, p.159.

6 Virginia Browne-Wilkinson, *Pepperrell Posterity*, Florence, 1982, pp.112–3.

7 Jules Prown has mapped Copley's Loyalist connections in London. See Jules Prown, *John Singleton Copley in England 1774–1815*, Cambridge, 1966, pp.260–261. Copley and Pepperrell had known each other in America, where they had quarrelled, but their shared situation resulted in an evident reconciliation.

8 Jules Prown, *John Singleton Copley in England 1774–1815*, Cambridge, 1966, cat.nos 359–361. For the other full compositional study see Anna Wells Rutledge, 'American Loyalists – A Drawing for a Noted Copley Group', *Art Quarterly XX (Summer 1957)*, pp.195–201.

9 Prown places the present sheet second in the chronology, after a slight study of the central figures noww in Boston (Prown, no.359). See Jules Prown, *John Singleton Copley in England 1774–1815*, Cambridge, 1966, p.266.

10 eds. Emily Ballew Neff and William L. Pressly, *John Singleton Copley in England,* exh.cat. Washington (National Gallery of Art), 1996, p.132.

11 Jules Prown, *John Singleton Copley in England 1774–1815*, Cambridge, 1966, p.265, no.15.

12 Joseph Wright of Derby visited Parma in 1775 and noted John Singleton Copley: 'has been hard at it five weeks & says he will be twice that time more over it but he will get it like the Original.' Elizabeth E. Barker, 'Documents Relating to Joseph Wright of Derby (1734 – 97)', *The Walpole* Society, 2009, LXXI, p.86. Copley reported to his mother on June 25 1775: 'I have begun my copy of the very fine Corregio, for which I have a commission from an English nobleman. I half dead-colou'd my copy, tho I have been here only one week.' On 22 August Copley reported the completion of the copy to his half-brother Henry Pelham. Eds. C. F. Adams, G. Jones and W. Ford, 1914, p.328 and 353. The nobleman was Richard, 1st Earl Grosvenor.

13 Ed. Robert Wark, *Sir Joshua Reynolds: Discourses on Art*, New Haven and London, 1975, p.29. Jules Prown identified the source of the central figures to be an engraving after Annibale Carracci. See Jules Prown, *John Singleton Copley in England 1774–1815*, Cambridge, 1966, p.266.

HUGH DOUGLAS HAMILTON 1739–1808

A lady wearing a pink turban

Pastel on laid paper
Oval 8⅞ × 7⅛ inches · 225 × 182 mm
Drawn late 1770s

COLLECTIONS
Private collection, USA, to 2014

Hugh Douglas Hamilton
Self-portrait, c.1791
Pastel and pencil
8⅞ × 6¾ inches · 225 × 170 mm
Photo © National Gallery of Ireland

This characteristic pastel portrait by the Irish artist Hugh Douglas Hamilton depicting a beautiful young woman in a pink turban survives in exceptionally fine preservation and allows us to judge his extraordinary skill as a portraitist in pastel.

Hugh Douglas Hamilton was born in Dublin, the son of a wig maker in Crow Street. He entered the Dublin Society School of Drawing about 1750 and studied under Robert West and James Mannin and was a pupil there for some eight years, winning three premiums for the best drawings of 1756. Hamilton probably left West's academy in the late 1750s and soon set up a flourishing business as a portraitist in pastels. Hamilton's small-scale, intimate pastel portraits were immensely popular. Their popularity rested on a combination of the luminous surface quality he achieved, the speed of execution (unlike oils, pastels required no drying time), portability and low cost. As a result of their popularity in 1764 Hamilton moved his practice to London, although he continued to preserve strong contacts with his native Ireland, returning periodically and sending works for exhibition at the Society of Artists in Dublin.

It was their comparatively inexpensiveness which was the most important factor in their popularity. Hamilton's average price for a small oval portrait was 9 guineas according to his earliest biographer Thomas Mulvany.[1] Compared with prices being charged by leading London portraitists for oil portraits (Joshua Reynolds was commanding up to 50 guineas for a half-length work during the 1770s). The present example, made just before Hamilton moved to Italy, perfectly reveals his working method.[2] Hamilton began by outlining the head and shoulders in

a light tone, he then, precisely as the pastellist John Russell notes, added the features in 'fint carmine tones' with touches of green used in the shadows. Hamilton then blended the tones on the face to produce the sitter's delicate complexion. He would then have added the background using the broad side of the pastel. Russell recommended certain colours for the background depending on the age of the sitter, blue was chosen as it contrasts with warm flesh tones of the face. In contrast to the finely drawn face, Hamilton has only blocked in the costume adding graphite lines to delineate certain aspects of the costume and to pick out the sitter's hair. The extraordinarily fine execution of the present portrait, its subtlety and its remarkable state of preservation underline Hamilton's ability as a pastellist.

NOTES

1   Thomas James Mulvany, 'Memoirs of Native Artists: Hugh Douglas Hamilton', *Dublin Monthly Magazine*, January 1842, p.69.

2   For a discussion of Hamilton's working method see Louise O'Connor, 'Hamilton's pastel portraits: materials and techniques', in ed. Anne Hodge, *Hugh Douglas Hamilton: A Life in Picutres*, exh.cat., Dublin (National Gallery of Ireland), 2008, pp.47–49.

GEORGE BARRET RA 1732–1784

Lake Ullswater: a party of tourists at the head of the lake

Gouache on paper laid down on linen
19 × 25½ inches · 482 × 647 mm
Signed and dated 'G Barret 22 February 1781'

COLLECTIONS
Private collection, 1986;
Desmond FitzGerald, Knight of Glin.

LITERATURE
Anne Crookshank and Desmond FitzGerald,
The Painters of Ireland c.1660–1920, London,
1978, p.119, pl.24;
Patricia Butler, *Three Hundred Years of Irish
Watercolours and Drawings*, London, 1990,
pp.52–55, pl.49;
Anne Crookshank and Desmond FitzGerald,
*The Watercolours of Ireland: Works on Paper in
Pencil, Pastel and Paint c.1600–1914*, London,
1994, pp.52–4, pl.56.

James Barry writing to the early theorist of
the sublime, Edmund Burke, noted that the
landscape painter George Barret:
*presents you with such a glorious assemblage, as
I have sometimes seen among high mountains
rising into unusual agreeable appearances while*

George Barret RA
Ullswater, Cumberland, c.1780
Gouache on paper laid down on linen
20 × 24 inches · 510 × 610 mm
National Gallery of Ireland, Dublin

*the early beams of the sun sport themselves …
through the vast arcades and sometimes glances
on a great lake whose ascending vapours spread
themselves like a veil over the distance.*[1]

This description of 'high mountains' and
'great lake' bathed in 'early beams of sun'
neatly describes Barret's impressive view
of Ullswater. In this gouache view a ferry
crosses the lake and a group of figures on
the right-hand of the composition picnick-
ing in a tent; Barret's view is therefore an
early celebration of the tourism to the area
stimulated by ideas of the picturesque.
Probably made for exhibition, the gouache
survives in remarkable preservation and has
been consistently praised as one of Barret's
most beautiful late works.[2]

George Barret was born in Ireland, where
he attended the Dublin Society drawing
schools under Robert West. While there
he coloured prints and in 1747 he won a
prize in the examination. He became a
friend of Edmund Burke, then a student
at Trinity College, Dublin and by tradition
it was Burke who introduced him to the
wild scenery of the Dargle valley and the
Powerscourt estate. In 1761 Barret moved to
London where he had moderate success as
a painter of estate views and idealised landscapes. By the date of the present powerful
view of Ullswater, Barret had fallen on hard
times and the following year Burke helped
secure his appointment as Master Painter to
the Chelsea Hospital.

This view of Ullswater was made on
a tour of the Lake District; in at least one
other picture from this trip is recorded. In
1781 Barret exhibited at the Royal Academy
a *View of Windermere Lake, in Westmoreland,
the effect, the sun beginning to appear in the
morning, with the mists breaking and dispersing*

(no.40). A gouache of a similar view of
Ullswater now in the National Gallery
of Ireland, Dublin was the source for an
engraving by Samuel Middiman for *Select
Views in Great Britain*. Barret has included an
elegant group of figures enjoying a picnic
on Soulby-Fell on the right of the composition; a ferry transports more tourists and
their horses across the lake to the base of
this hill. Tourism to the Lakes was gaining
in popularity during the last decades of the
century to the extent that it formed a subject
for Wordsworth's scorn in *The Brothers*
published in 1800.[3]

Barret usually worked in oil, but here is
working in gouache, a medium which by
this date was losing ground in popularity
to watercolour. Rather than concentrating
on the naturalism of the view, Barret has
focused on the monumental grandeur and
effects of light, emphasising the unreal
qualities of sublime landscape. Painted at the
end of a tradition of gouache painting which
had begun with Marco Ricci in Britain, this
remarkably well preserved and monumental
view represents an unexpected combination
of carefully structured topography and
sublimity and ranks as perhaps the finest
example of a landscape in gouache executed
in Britain at the period.

NOTES
1 Ed. Edward Fryer, *The Works of James Barry,
   Esq.*, London, 1809, 1. p.16.
2 Anne Crookshank and Desmond FitzGerald,
   *The Watercolours of Ireland: Works on Paper in
   Pencil, Pastel and Paint c.1600–1914*, London,
   1994, pp.52–4.
3 John Murdoch, *The Discovery of the Lake
   District: A Northern Arcadia and its Uses*, exh.
   cat., London, 1984, p.27.

FRANCIS TOWNE 1739–1816

Lake Albano

Pen and grey ink and brown wash, watermark 'J WHATMAN'
12½ × 18 inches · 318 × 457 mm
Signed, inscribed, dated and numbered: 'No 2
Lake of Albano / Evening Sun behind the trees
on the left / hand / july the 10th 1781 / Francis
Towne' and further inscribed: 'A copy of
this painted on canvas [sic] the same size for
James Curtis Esq. 1784' (on the verso)

COLLECTIONS
Francis Towne;
James White (1744–1825), Exeter, by bequest
from the above in 1816;
John Herman Merivale (1779–1844), Barton
Place, Exeter, by reversion as residuary
legatee on White's death in 1825;
Maria Sophia Merivale (1853–1928) and Judith
Ann Merivale (1860–1945), grand-daughters
of the above, Oxford, by descent May 1915,
(Barton Place inventory no.23);
Squire Gallery, acquired from Judith Ann
Merivale, 1933 for £6 10s;
Leonard G Duke, acquired from the above,
February 1934, for 16½ gns (D105);
Nigel Warren QC (1912–67), acquired from the
above, November 1955, £200;
And by descent to 2002;
Private collection, USA, 2014.

LITERATURE
Royal Albert Memorial Museum, *Three Exeter
Artists of the Eighteenth Century*, exh.cat.,
Exeter, Festival of Britain, 1951, no.188.

EXHIBITED
Exeter, Royal Albert Memorial Museum,
Three Exeter Artists of the Eighteenth Century,
Festival of Britain, 1951, no.188.

When Francis Towne travelled to Rome in
1780 at the age of forty, he joined a colony
of British painters who were exploring the
Italian countryside and forging new modes
of landscape painting. Towne in turn, during
his brief year-long tour, developed a singular
approach in his watercolours; he produced
highly linear, on-the-spot drawings, which
he later strengthened with ink and wash,
preferring monochrome washes to bright
colours. His views, whilst topographical,
focus on the generalised masses of buildings
and vegetation, rather than the minutiae
of detail. Towne responded to the shifting
Italian light producing a clarity of vision
very unlike the diffuse, Romantic works of
his contemporaries, John Robert Cozens or
Thomas Jones. In the summer of 1781 Towne
travelled into the countryside around Rome
and produced a number of striking images
of the classic Grand Tour sites – including

views of Tivoli, Frascati and the lakes of
Albano and Nemi – he also produced a
number of remarkably concentrated studies
of vegetation. The present view of *Lake
Albano*, whilst depicting the famous lake in
the Castelli Romani, focusses principally on
the evening light falling through trees and
demonstrates Towne's remarkable technical
virtuosity in handling wash.

Thomas Jones writing in 1776 of his first
visit to Lake Albano noted:
*This walk considered with respect to its
classic locality, the Awful marks of the modern
Specimens of Art, and the various extensive
& delightful prospects it commands is, to the
Scholar, naturalist, Antiquarian and Artist,
without doubt, The most pleasing and interesting in the Whole World – And here I can not
help observing with what new and uncommon
Sensations I was filled on my first traversing this
beautiful and picturesque Country – Every scene
seemed anticipated in some dream – It appeared
Magick Land.*[1]

The idea of the landscape of the Roman
Campagna being a place of new and exciting views and simultaneously familiar is
something consistently commented upon
by travellers in the eighteenth century. For
Jones, and Towne, Lake Albano, fringed by
the towns of Castel Gandolfo and Albano
would have been 'anticipated' in the works
of the seventeenth-century painters,
Claude and Gaspard Dughet, as well as the
pictures of Richard Wilson and their own
contemporaries.[2] Towne would therefore

Francis Towne
Chestnut Grove, Rocca del Papa, near Lake Albano, 1781
Grey wash and black ink and watercolour over pencil
15¼ × 10 inches · 387 × 254 mm
Signed, inscribed and dated
Yale Center for British Art, New Haven

have approached this new landscape with a number of compositional preconceptions. Towne chose a conventional position for the present view. Seated on the Galleria di Sopra, the road that runs around Lake Albano, looking west across the lake towards the town of Castel Gandolfo and Rome beyond. This was a celebrated view made by numerous visiting British artists, including Jones but most spectacularly and numerously by John Robert Cozens. But rather than showing the distinctive dome of Bernini's San Tommaso in Castel Gandolfo and the sweeping line of the lake, Towne has focused on the evening light falling through the trees.

The woods which fringed the lakes of Albano and Nemi evidently appealed to Towne as he executed a number of

Francis Towne
Lake Albano with Castel Gandolfo, 1781
Watercolour, with pen and ink, on two conjoined sheets
12⅝ × 22½ inches · 321 × 702 mm
Signed and dated: 'No 7 Francis Towne delt July 12 1781'
© The Trustees of the British Museum

John Robert Cozens
The Galleria di Sopra, Lake Albano, 1780s
Pencil and watercolour
17 × 24¼ inches · 432 × 616 mm
Private collection, USA (formerly with Lowell Libson Ltd)

exceptionally compelling studies of trees in the area. A grey and black wash drawing inscribed 'Taken in a wood near Albano' is in the Oppé collection in the Tate and other drawings show chestnut trees in the woods around Rocca di Papa, a village on the hills above Lake Albano.[3] In both the Rocca di Papa views and the Albano view Towne switched from using the brown washes he had been employing in Rome, back to the cooler grey tones he had used before his departure for the Continent. One explanation for Towne's interest in the woods of the Castelli Romani and the number of studies he made on his tour of the lakes in July 1781 might have been the scarcity of trees in Rome itself. Contemporaries frequently commented on the barren landscape and the poor quality of the agricultural land close to the city.[4] It may also be that Towne felt less pressure to draw, what Jones called, 'the Awful marks of the modern Specimens of Art' – Bernini's churches at Castel Gandolfo and Ariccia – than the antiquities of classical Rome and therefore concentrate on studies of trees and the bright Italian summer light rather than the specific landmarks of his views.

Towne did make other views of Albano which are closer in spirit and topographical specificity to the more traditional views of Castel Gandolfo. A large, coloured panorama of *Lake Albano* is preserved in the Towne albums in the British Museum. But in the present drawing Towne is principally interested in the quality of the evening light falling through the trees. Towne has used only minimal drawn lights to create the setting, profiling the outlines of the trees and suggesting the receding hills in the background; the rest of the sheet is created using carefully controlled washes. The alternating shadows and shafts of light are evoked solely with different strengths of grey wash giving a strong sense of design to Towne's composition.

Towne noted on the reverse of the

drawing that he painted an oil version of the subject for James Curtis who also ordered a view of L'Arriccia. According to Richard Stephens, Curtis was a brewer and merchant of Old South Sea House, Broad Street, London, who was an executor and leading beneficiary of the will of Towne's long-standing acquaintance Samuel Edwards. It is interesting that he should have commissioned a pair of views of the two adjacent towns, Ariccia and Albano, suggesting that despite the limited topographical appeal of the present view, it was still an effective evocation of the 'Magick land' of Grand Tour Italy. The present drawing passed along with many of his other works in 1816 to his friend James White of Exeter, on whose death it passed to Towne's residuary legatee John Herman Merivale. Sold by Merivale's descendants it belonged to the distinguished collector Lenoard Duke in the beginning of the twentieth century. The present drawing demonstrates the artistic innovation of Towne's continental work, with its subtle use of light, monochrome palette and sense of design it is a powerful example of his response to the Italian landscape.

We are very grateful to Richard Stephens for his help with the provenance of the present drawing and for sharing his research on James Curtis.

NOTES

1 Ed. P. Oppé, 'Memoirs of Thomas Jones, Penkerrig, Radnorshire, 1803', *The Walpole Society*, vol.32, 1946–8, p.55.

2 See Francis Hawcroft, *Travels in Italy 1776–1783*, exh.cat. Manchester (Whitworth Art Gallery), 1988.

3 Timothy Wilcox, *Francis Towne*, exh.cat. London (Tate), 1997, pp.73–74.

4 For an account of the agriculture of Lazio in the eighteenth century see Hans Gross, *Rome in the Age of Enlightenment: The Post Tridentine System the Ancien Regime*, Cambridge, 1990, pp.175–195.

THOMAS ROWLANDSON 1756–1827

Animal Magnetism – the Centre of Attention

Pen and ink and watercolour
15³⁄₁₆ × 11½ inches · 385 × 293mm
Inscribed: 'Animal Magnetism. The Centre of attention'
Drawn c.1790

COLLECTIONS
Thomas Capron, Arundel House,
Richmond, by 1880;
Private collection, UK, to 2006;
Private collection, UK, 2014.

LITERATURE
Joseph Grego, *Rowlandson the Caricaturist*,
1880, vol.II, p.426.

EXHIBITED
London, Lowell Libson Ltd, *Beauty and the Beast: A loan exhibition of Rowlandson's works from British private collections*, 2007, no.16.

Thomas Rowlandson was one of the most vibrant and dextrous draughtsman of the eighteenth century and this large sheet is one of his finest works of satire. The composition presents a compendium of caricature heads that fascinated Rowlandson throughout his career, pressing their attention on a beautiful young woman. The title, *Animal Magnetism*, is an allusion to a contemporary scientific theory and anchors this drawing in contemporary satire of the 1780s.

The title of this drawing refers to the popular theories of a German doctor, Franz Mesmer. Mesmer published his theory of 'Animal Magnetism' which postulated the existence of an invisible natural force exerted by animals. He believed that the force could have physical effects, including healing. Mesmer and his followers believed that the world was filled with 'fluid matter'

Thomas Rowlandson
The Opera Singers, c.1790–5
Watercolour with pen and black ink over graphite
5½ × 4 1⁄₁₆ inches' 140 × 119 mm
Yale Center for British Art, Paul Mellon Collection

Animal Magnetism The Centre of attraction

which 'as all the bodies moving in the world, abound with pores, this fluid matter introduces itself through the interstices and returns backwards and forwards, flowing through one body by the currents which issue there from another, as in a magnet.'[1] Adherents of the theory suggested that this 'fluid matter' needed to be in equilibrium, any imbalance caused illness, which could be treated with a form of hypnotism. The most successful mesmerist in London was J. B. Mainauduc, who had purchased a medical degree after study with William Hunter. Many fashionable patients were 'Mesmerised' including Georgiana, Duchess of Devonshire who was thrown into hysterics by the experience, Lady Salisbury who was put to sleep and the Prince of Wales.

As both popularity and skepticism increased, many became convinced that animal magnetism could lead to sexual exploitation of women. Not only did the practice involve close personal contact via the waving of hands over the body, but people were concerned that the animal magnetists could hypnotize women and direct them at will. The playwright Elizabeth Inchbald wrote the farce *Animal Magnetism* in 1788 in which she parodied mesmerism; in it the 'doctor' affirms that he can, if he pleases, make every woman who comes near him fall in love with him.

In this drawing Rowlandson neatly inverts this fear. Rather than the mesmeric doctor exploiting the defenseless woman, Rowlandson shows a voluptuous and fashionably dressed woman at the center of a male throng evidently exerting her own 'animal magnetism' over her male admirers. The 'center of attention' recalls Rowlandson's depictions of famous actresses of the day,

the ostrich feather headdress reappearing in numerous drawings of modish, attractive and celebrity women, for example *the Opera Singers* in the Yale Center for British Art. The admirers represent the full kaleidoscope of figures Rowlandson satirized in his drawings, from the idealized youth on the left which is frequently read as a form of self-portrait, to the rubicund old man with bulbous nose and glasses in the bottom right. The topic was one designed to appeal to Rowlandson, who frequently explored the animalistic qualities of humans in the albums he produced entitled: *Studies in Comparative Anatomy, Resemblances between the Countenances of Men and Beasts*. Rowlandson's literal interpretation of Mesmer's term is demonstrated in the physiognomies of some of the admirers, for example the figure in the bottom left which appears distinctly porcine in his features.

Thomas Rowlandson
Comparative physiognomy: studies of heads, c.1825
Pen and ink on paper · 8½ × 6¾ inches · 216 × 172 mm
Carnegie Museum of Art (formerly Lowell Libson Ltd)

NOTE

1 Wonders and mysteries of animal magnetism displayed; or the history, art, practice, and progress of that useful science, from its first rise in the city of Paris, to the present time. With several Curious Cases and new Anecdotes of the Principal Professors, London, 1791, pp.11–12.

JOSEPH MALLORD WILLIAM TURNER RA 1775–1851

The Road between Caserta and the Aqueduct

Watercolour with traces of pencil
5⅞ × 9⅛ inches · 150 × 232 mm
Painted *c.*1794–5

COLLECTIONS

The Ven. Archdeacon Charles Burney by
1887, (d.1907);
Misses M. and J. Burney, by descent;
Thomas Agnew & Sons, 1991;
Private collection, acquired from the above,
to 2014.

EXHIBITED

London, Royal Academy, *Works by the Old
Masters*, Winter 1887, (ex-catalogue);
London, Agnew's, *118th Annual Exhibition
of English Watercolours and Drawings*, 1991,
no.7, repr.;
Oxford, Ashmolean Museum, *For the Love
of Drawing: Drawings from an Oxfordshire
Private Collection*, 2002, no.37.

This finely executed and well preserved
watercolour by Turner offers important
evidence of his fascination with earlier
British artists, particularly the works of
the pioneering watercolourist John Robert
Cozens. Almost certainly painted whilst

John Robert Cozens
*From the Road Between Caserta and the
Aqueduct, 1782*
Watercolour and pencil
14½ × 21 inches · 370 × 534 mm
Whitworth Art Gallery, University of Manchester

Turner had access to works by Cozens
belonging to the physician and collector Dr
Thomas Monro, it also demonstrates how
important Italy was to Turner even before
his first visit in 1819.

In 1792 Turner entered the schools of
the Royal Academy where he drew from
casts after the antique and from life models.
However, landscape and topographical
drawing and painting were not taught at the
Academy, and in this vital area Turner was
in many ways his own teacher, except for
the encouragement and help provided by Dr
Thomas Monro at his informal 'academy'.
Monro, a physician who specialized in
mental disorders, was a considerable collector and amateur artist who from about 1794
encouraged young artists to visit his house
in the Adelphi to copy from drawings in his
collection, many of them by Cozens, who
spent the last years of his life in the doctor's
care. Turner's close contemporary and
friend Thomas Girtin was among his fellow
students at the Adelphi.[1] Our most detailed
information about the Monro academy
comes from the diary of Joseph Farington,
who first mentioned it in December 1794 and
then recorded on 12 November 1798 that:
*Turner & Girtin told us that they had been
employed by Dr. Monro 3 years to draw at his
house in the evenings ... Turner afterwards told
me that Dr. Munro had been a material friend to
him, as well as to Girtin.*[2]

The present work is, with variations,
based on a much larger watercolour by John
Robert Cozens, now in the Whitworth Art
Gallery, Manchester. Cozens visited Italy for
the second time with the great patron and
collector William Beckford in 1782–3 when
they made an extensive tour in the South of
the country. Beckford and Cozens visited in

November 1782 and a pencil study for the
watercolour is preserved in the Beckford
sketchbooks in the Whitworth.[3]

At Munro's 'Academy' young artists were
encouraged to use works in his collection
as the basis for their own works. A number
of wash and watercolour drawings by
Turner exist to testify to his fascination with
Cozens and these range from very loose
approximations of Cozens's compositions to
more closely observed exercises replicating
the structures of Cozens's watercolours.
They are, however, never direct copies in
the conventional sense as Turner always
used them as a basis to express his own very
different artistic voice. In the present work
Turner carefully approximated Cozens's
treatment of the view particularly in the
construction of the foreground and receding
landscape albeit on a considerably smaller
scale, underlining his mastery of the devel-
oping technique of watercolour of which
he, even at an early stage was the master.
Whilst Cozens's interest in the view was to
emphasize the dramatic almost theatrical
aspects of the view, Turner, by reducing
the format of the composition found in
the Cozens, placed more emphasis on the
mountains in the distance.

NOTES

1   For the Monro Academy see Andrew Wilton,
    'The Monro School Question: Some Answers',
    Turner Studies, vol.4, no.2, pp.8–23.
2   eds..Kenneth Garlick and Angus Macintyre,
    The Diary of Joseph Farington, New Haven and
    London, 1979, III, p.1090.
3   Francis Hawcroft, *Travels in Italy: 1776–1783,
    based on the Memoirs of Thomas Jones*, exh.cat.
    Manchester (Whitworth Art Gallery), 1988,
    no.86.

SIR THOMAS LAWRENCE PRA 1769–1830

A life drawing

Black, red and white chalks on buff paper
13½ × 9½ inches · 342 × 242 mm
Drawn *c.*1789–90

COLLECTIONS
Possibly Lawrence's posthumous sale,
Christie's, *A catalogue of The Remaining
Pictures and Unfinished Sketches of Sir Thomas
Lawrence*, 18 June 1831;
Walter Brandt, 1998;
Private collection.

This finely executed chalk drawing of a life
model posed as the Crouching Venus was
probably made by Thomas Lawrence at the
Royal Academy Schools. Lawrence entered
the Academy Schools in 1787 and although
we are told he only remained a student for a
short period of time, would have continued
to have access to the model which was posed
nightly at the Life Academy. This highly
modelled study is part of a series of drawings which Lawrence made sometime before
he was elected an Associate Academician
in 1791 and is likely to be identified with
a lot of drawings included in Lawrence's
posthumous auction in 1830.[1] Surviving life
drawings by Lawrence are exceptionally rare
making this early sheet a significant addition.

Lawrence's contemporary, the painter
Henry Howard, recorded his first impres-
sions of the young Lawrence at the Royal
Academy:
*His proficiency in drawing, even at that time, was
such as to leave all his competitors in the antique
school far behind him. His personal attractions
were as remarkable as his talent: altogether he
excited a great sensation, and seemed, to the
admiring students, as nothing less than a young
Raphael suddenly dropt among them. He was
very handsome; and his chestnut locks flowing on
his shoulders, gave him a romantic appearance.*[2]

Lawrence's early biographer D.E.
Williams observed that Lawrence:
*made, however, but two or three drawings in the
Academy, which were executed with a black-lead
pencil on white paper, elaborately tinted down,
till the high light had the effect of white put on,
rather than of the paper left; a style at that time
novel, or at least not practised in the school. Two
drawings of the Gladiator Repellens, and of the
Belvidere Apollo, were deemed very accurate and
beautiful.*[3]

The first Academicians made surpris-
ingly few rules governing the education of
students, other than the requirement that a
student have a drawing or model approved
for admission and again to progress into the
Life Academy. Students were admitted for
a term of six years, this was later altered to
seven years and then to ten. But this was
in no way regarded as the duration of a
course of study but merely a statement of
eligibility to use the Academy's facilities and
to compete for prizes. The timetable itself
was fairly minimal, following the traditional
model in which the purpose of an Academy
was to provide instruction in draughtsmanship and theory while the student learned
their chosen art of painting, sculpture or
architecture with a master. The Antique or
Plaister Academy was open from 9am to 3
pm with a 2 hour session in the evening. The
Life Academy, however, consisted of only a 2
hour class each night.

This drawing seems likely to have
been made from a posed model in the
Life Academy in Somerset House. The
Visitor would set the model and Lawrence
would have studied under a number of
Academicians including Henry Fuseli and
James Barry. There was a long tradition in
European academies of posing the model
to emulate a piece of classical sculpture.
When J.M.W. Turner became Visitor in
1812 he became famous for this practice.
Redgrave recorded that Turner: 'when a
visitor in the life school he introduced a
capital practice, which it is to be regretted
has not been continued: he chose for study a
model as nearly as possible corresponding in
form and character with some fine antique
figure, which he placed by the side of the
model posed in the same action.'[4] This was
likely to have been happening earlier as the
present drawing shows a model posed as
the Crouching Venus, or Vénus Accroupie
a sculpture in the Louvre. Unlike the
technique described by Williams, Lawrence
has used the classic method of *trois crayons*,
adding red to black and white chalk to
capture the flesh tones. Lawrence was to
refine this use of red highlighting in the
sophisticated portrait drawings that became
an occasional feature of his mature career.

NOTES

1 The present drawing is related to a pair of
 studies by Lawrence of the same model seen
 from slightly different angels; the drawings
 were purchased from Lawrence's posthumous
 sale in 1830 by Sir Charles Greville and sold
 by his descendants at Sotheby's 5 April, 1973,
 lot 85.
2 D.E. Williams, *The Life and Correspondence
 of Sir Thomas Lawrence*, London, 1831, 1, p.99.
3 D.E. Williams, *The Life and Correspondence
 of Sir Thomas Lawrence*, London, 1831, 1, p.99.
4 Richard and Samuel Redgrave, *A Century
 of British Painters*, London, 1981, p.256.

JOHN FLAXMAN RA 1755–1826

Orestes Standing over the Bodies of Clytemnestra and Aegisthus

Pencil, strengthened with ink
8 × 11½ inches · 203 × 292 mm
Drawn *c.*1795

COLLECTIONS
Thomas Hope, acquired from the artist;
Lord Francis Hope Pelham-Clinton-Hope by
descent, 1917;
Pelham-Clinton-Hope sale, Humbert &
Flint, 1917;
Scott & Fowles, New York by 1918;
Private collection, USA.

LITERATURE
Martin Birnbaum (ed.), *Catalogue of an
Exhibition of Original Drawings by John
Flaxman RA*, Scott & Fowles, New York, 1918,
no.60 ('Orestes), p.31.

EXHIBITED
New York, Scott & Fowles, 1918, *Exhibition
of Original Drawings by John Flaxman RA*, 1918,
no.60 ('Orestes).
Pencil, strengthened with ink

JOHN FLAXMAN RA 1755–1826

Oceanus and Prometheus Bound

9 × 11¼ inches · 229 × 285 mm
Signed 'J Flaxman' (pasted on
border, lower right)
Drawn *c*.1795

COLLECTIONS
Thomas Hope, acquired from the artist;
Lord Francis Hope Pelham-Clinton-Hope by
descent, 1917;
Pelham-Clinton-Hope sale, Humbert &
Flint, 1917;
Scott & Fowles, New York by 1918;
Private collection, USA.

LITERATURE
Martin Birnbaum (ed.), *Catalogue of an
Exhibition of Original Drawings by John
Flaxman RA*, Scott & Fowles, New York, 1918,
no.58 ('Oceanus (Prometheus chained)', p.31.

EXHIBITED
New York, Scott & Fowles, 1918, *Exhibition
of Original Drawings by John Flaxman RA*,
1918, no.58 ('Oceanus (Prometheus chained)'.

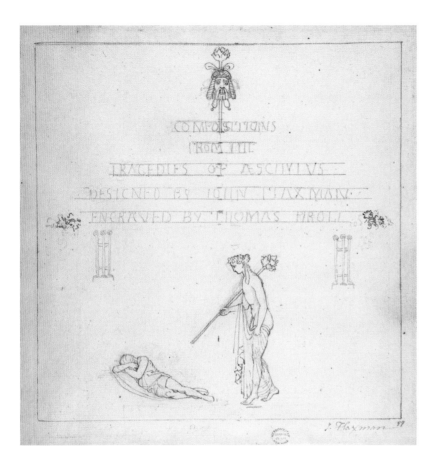

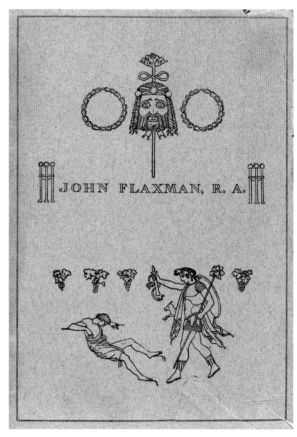

These line drawings were made by John Flaxman in preparation for his illustrations to *Aeschylus* commissioned in Rome in 1792 by Margaret, Countess Spencer. Flaxman's outline drawings were recognised immediately as revolutionary, despite their origin in the reproduction of Greek vase paintings, in their purity of outline and narrative clarity; as David Bindman has observed: 'their influence on nineteenth-century artists is incalculable'.[1] The sheets are two from a series of 70 drawings which were acquired by Flaxman's early patron, Thomas Hope and which, following their sale from Hope's Surrey house, The Deepdene, formed the focus of the first dedicated exhibition of Flaxman's work in America, in New York in 1918.[2]

The two drawings depict scenes from the plays of Aeschylus. The first *Orestes standing over the bodies of Clytemnestra and Aegisthus* and the second *Oceanus with Prometheus Chained*; scenes which both appeared in the engravings produced by Tommaso Piroli in 1795 which were published by Flaxman himself. The series of drawing from Aeschylus was the third such project Flaxman undertook. The first was likely to have been his illustrations to Homer commissioned by Mrs Hare Naylor, the second illustrations to Dante commissioned by Thomas Hope probably sometime in

1792. Hope's relationship with Flaxman was clearly a close one, he also acquired a major figural group *Aurora Abducting Cephalus* from Flaxman in Rome in 1792, now in the Lady Lever Art Gallery, Liverpool.[3] It is likely that the present drawings were acquired by Hope – along with the rest of the album – from Flaxman whilst he was designing the illustrations to *Dante*.

Flaxman chose scenes from all surviving plays by Aeschylus, placing the emphasis on *Prometheus*. The first drawing shows Oceanus arriving to placate Promeheus. Flaxman designed a classical river god close in type to the Roman sculpture of a *River god* from the Museo Capitolino, with Oceanus's legs neatly encircled by the animal's tail. The continuous sequence of curves formed by the beast's neck, belly and tail create a surface pattern which is both elegant and in deliberate contrast to the jarring lines of the struggling Prometheus. August Wilhelm von Schlegel writing on Flaxman in 1799 regarded the illustrations to Aeschylus his greatest works, particularly admiring his plate of Oceanus, which he noted: 'looks so marvellous that one does not ask if the poet's intention is being pursued, where in fact the animal is a four-footed bird.'[4] The second drawing depicts Orestes standing over the bodies of his mother Clytemnestra and Aegisthus, the man who had murdered his father, Agamemnon and seduced his mother. The stark linearity recalls Greek vase painting and the primitive quality of contemporary neo-classicism, whilst the evident emotional intensity of the scene suggests the context of Romanticism.

Amongst the group of drawings acquired by the New York dealers Scott and Fowles from The Deepdene were drawings from each of Flaxman's illustrated series. The majority were of Homeric subjects but 13 were from Dante and Aeschylus; they included frontispieces to both the Dante series – acquired by Greville Winthrop and now in the Fogg Art Museum – and Aeschylus which was acquired by the Metropolitan Museum of Art, New York. The pioneering show held at 590 Fifth Avenue was mounted by Scott and Fowles's principal partner Martin Birnbaum who wrote a notable introduction to the catalogue, praising Flaxman and Hope stating that the drawings: 'afford a kind of standard by which any artist might take the measure of his graphic ability' suggesting this was something 'the power of Van Gogh, the theoretical importance of Picasso, and the dignified failures of the post-impressionists have temporarily blinded us to obvious beauty.'[5] It was evidently a commercial success and numerous Flaxman drawings entered distinguished private and public collections. Scott & Fowles donated three to the Metropolitan Museum of Art who had acquired a further three and would be given a fourth in 1952.

NOTES

1 David Bindman, 'Thomas Hope's Modern Sculptures: 'a zealous and liberal patronage of its contemporary professors', in Ed. David Watkin and Philip Hewat-Jaboor, *Thomas Hope: Regency Designer*, exh.cat. London (Victoria & Albert Museum), 2008, p.134.

2 Scott & Fowles, *Catalogue of an Exhibition of Original Drawings by John Flaxman RA*, New York, 1918.

3 Ed. David Watkin and Philip Hewat-Jaboor, *Thomas Hope: Regency Designer*, exh.cat. London (Victoria & Albert Museum), 2008, no.55, p.352.

4 Quoted in David Irwin, *John Flaxman 1755–1826: Sculptor, Illustrator, Designer*, London, 1979, p.88.

5 Scott & Fowles, *Catalogue of an Exhibition of Original Drawings by John Flaxman RA*, New York, 1918, p.28.

WILLIAM BLAKE 1757–1827

The Virgin Hushing the Young John the Baptist

Pen and ink and oil on paper on linen, laid
down on canvas
10⅝ × 15 inches · 270 × 380 mm
Signed with monogram and dated 1799
(lower left)

COLLECTIONS

Thomas Butts, commissioned from the
artist;
Thomas Butts, Jr., son of the above;
Francis Turner Palgrave, by 1863;
Edward William Hooper, Cambridge,
Massachusetts, by 1880;
Mrs. John Briggs Potter, daughter of the
above;
Mrs. John B. Swann, daughter of the above;
Warren Howell, 1975;
Private collection, USA, 1977 to 2015.

After Studio of Raphael
La Vierge au voile
Etching and engraving on chine collé, *c.*1840–64
© The Trustees of the British Museum

LITERATURE

William Michael Rossetti, *Annotated
Catalogue of Blake's Pictures and Drawings*, in:
Alexander Gilchrist, *Life of William Blake*, 2
vols., London 1863, p.230, no.184;
William Michael Rossetti, *Annotated
Catalogue of Blake's Pictures and Drawings*, in:
Alexander Gilchrist, Life of William Blake,
2 vols., London 1880, p.243, no.210;
Geoffrey Keynes, *William Blake's Illustrations
to the Bible*, London 1957, p.30, no.99;
David Bindman, *Blake as an Artist*, Oxford
1977, pp.122 f. and 129, pl.101;
Martin Butlin, *The Paintings and Drawings
of William Blake*, 2 vols., New Haven &
London 1981, vol.1, p.327, no.406, vol.2,
pl.491;
David Bindman (ed.), *William Blake. His Art
and Times*, exh.cat., 1982, no.70, color pl.IX.

EXHIBITED

Boston, Museum of Fine Arts, *Drawings,
Water Colors, Old Engravings by William Blake*,
June 1880, no.2;
Boston, Museum of Fine Arts, Print
Department, *Books, Water Colors, Engravings,
Etc. by William Blake*, February-March 1891,
no.13;
New Haven, Yale Center for British Art &
Toronto, Art Gallery of Ontario, *William
Blake. His Art and Times*, 1982–83, no.70;
Tokyo, National Museum of Western Art,
William Blake, 1990, no.47;
New York, Salander-O'Reilly Galleries,
*William Blake. Paintings, Watercolors and
Drawings*, New York, 1992, no.3 (on loan).

William Blake's exceptional painting of
The Virgin Hushing the Young John the Baptist
comes from a series of fifty paintings
commissioned in 1799 by Blake's most significant patron, Thomas Butts. This small work
survives in remarkable condition; unlike
the majority of Blake's paintings in tempera
which have suffered severe deterioration. In
this series Blake used a glue-based watercolour medium, and the fact that the present
work was painted directly onto paper rather
than on canvas or copper like the majority
of the others helped to keep it stable. The
striking, sinuousness of the composition
and the eccentric interpretation of the
subject-matter offer perfect illustrations of
Blake's conceptual and technical inventiveness and his fascination with design. Only
about thirty of the Butts pictures survive and
only a handful remain in private collections
making this one of the most important and
best preserved of Blake's paintings to appear
in recent years.

Thomas Butts was a clerk in the office
of the Commissary General of Musters and
would become a consistent and important
patron of Blake.

As Gilchrist noted:

*One consistent patron there was … without
his friendly countenance, even less would have
remain to show the world, or a portion of it,
what manner of man Blake was. I man Mr.
Thomas Butts, whose long friendship with Blake
commenced at this period. For nearly thirty years
he continued (with few interruptions) a steady
buyer at moderate prices of Blake's drawings,
temperas, and frescoes; the only large buyer the
artiest ever had. Occasionally he would take of
Blake a drawing a week. He, in this way, often
supplied the imaginative man with the bare
means of subsistence when no others existed – at*

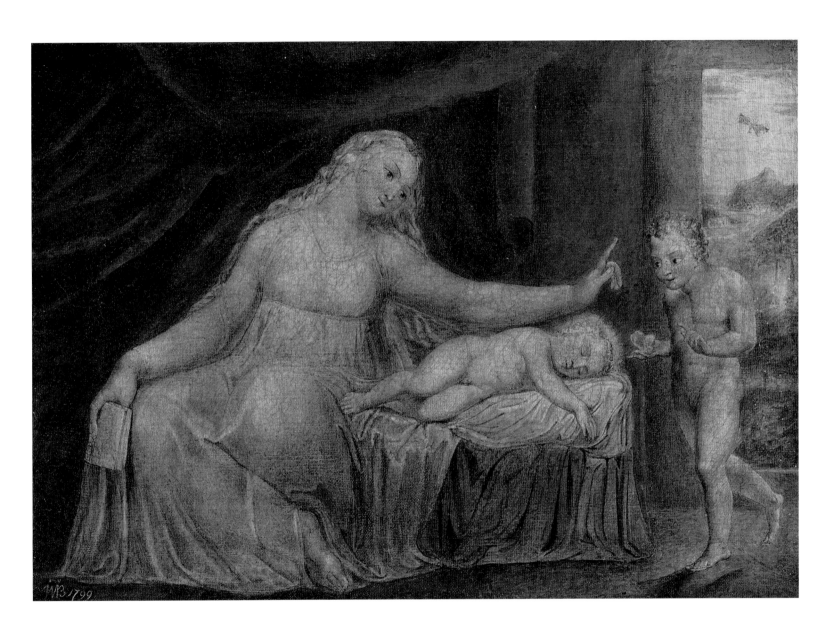

all events from his art. All honour to the solitary appreciator and to his zealous constancy! As years rolled by, Mr Butts' house in in Fitzroy Square became a perfect Blake Gallery.[1]

The perfect 'Blake Gallery' contained the fifty illustrations to the Bible as well as over eighty watercolours of Biblical Subjects.[2] Butts paid Blake steadily for pictures and lessons to teach his son engraving until about 1816.[3] Butts's commission provided Blake with considerable freedom to develop his pictorial style and the tempera paintings provided a vehicle for his imagination and personal theology. Blake himself characterized the commission as a 'Miracle', writing in August 1799 to George Cumberland describing the commission from Thomas Butts for 'Fifty small Pictures' of subjects from the Bible:

As to myself, about whom you are so kindly Interested, I live by Miracle. I am Painting small Pictures from the Bible. For as to Engraving, in which art I cannot reproach myself with any neglect, yet I am laid by in a corner as if I did not Exist... My Work pleases my employer, & I have an order for Fifty small Pictures at One Guinea

each, which is Something better than mere copying after another artist. But above all, I feel myself happy & contented.[4]

The present painting was one of ten completed in 1799, the first year of the commission. The painting shows the infant John the Baptist eagerly entering a room to show the sleeping Christ child a butterfly that he holds in his hand. Jesus has just fallen asleep, after the Virgin has read to him, and she admonishes John to be silent. Her outstretched finger at the same time points in the direction of another butterfly in the sky. Rather than being a Biblical episode, the subject-matter relates to a passage in Apocryphal writing, but as David Bindman has pointed out it was a subject-matter familiar in Italian Renaissance painting, known as the 'Madonna del Silenzio.'[5] As such it belongs to a group of Blake's paintings which have Marion iconography and look towards Italian old master's for their subject-matter and inspiration.

The most famous 'Madonna del Silenzio' is the work from Raphael's studio *The Madonna of the Blue Diadem* now in the

Louvre. The painting was well known in Britain through numerous engravings and the composition, as well as the subject-matter, seems to have influenced Blake. The Louvre painting shows the Virgin, head inclined, arm outstretched, with the Christ child asleep and a mountainous landscape beyond. Raphael's composition has traditionally been read as exploring the theme of Christ's future sacrifice, which is alluded to by the shroud-like cloth on which he sleeps; the Virgin's action in silencing the infant St John has been read as cautioning him not to awaken Christ to his Passion before his time. Blake may have been aware of the painting of the same theme by Annibale Carracci, in the Royal Collection which was engraved by Francesco Bartolozzi. Blake's reliance on Renaissance and Baroque paintings as both an iconographic and visual source has not been fully explored. But it seems that other paintings designed for Butts respond to earlier masters. Martin Butlin has pointed out that the subject-matter of *The Christ Child Asleep on a Cross* may derive from a painting by Guido Reni which was visible in

William Blake *Zacharias and the Angel, 1799–1800*
Pen and black ink, tempera and glue size on canvas · 10½ × 15 inches · 267 × 381 mm
Signed with monogram, lower left · Metropolitan Museum of Art, New York, Bequest of William Church Osborn, 1951 (acc. no.: 51.30.1)
© The Metropolitan Museum of Art / Art Resource / Scala, Florence, 2014

William Blake *The Adoration of the Kings, 1799*
Tempera on canvas
10⅛ × 14⅝ inches · 257 × 371 mm
Signed with monogram and dated 1799, lower right
Royal Pavilion, Libraries & Museums, Brighton and Hove

London at the sale of the Orléans collection in 1798.[6] David Bindman has suggested that the figure of Christ is related to 'the pose of Michelangelo's lost sculpture of a *Sleeping Cupid*' probably destroyed in the 17th century but echoed in later representations.[7] Blake has, therefore, drawn together and absorbed a whole range of references to earlier art; as he himself said in the same year, his figures were 'those of Michael Angelo, Rafael & the Antique, & of the best living Models.'[8] Such a considered use of Renaissance and Baroque sources gives Blake's compositions a grandeur despite its modest size.

The theme of the passion and resurrection is further alluded to by Blake's most unusual iconographical inclusion: the butterflies. The butterflies, one being brought by the young John the Baptist to show the sleeping Christ and another flying over the landscape visible through the open door, are immediately suggestive of a pagan context. As David Bindman has suggested their presence refers to the legend of Psyche, who was often represented with or by a butterfly, in the words of a contemporary poet, 'The symbol of the soul's immortal flight.'[9] Blake's own poetry and illustrations are filled with references to the butterfly as a symbol for the resurrection of the soul. For example in Blake's illustration to Young's *Night Thoughts* Blake adds above his depiction of Christ healing a youth a butterfly risen from a corpse. The butterfly in the landscape may well be read as a symbol of the resurrection, continuing the allusion to the Passion and Christ's future suffering. The butterflies also offer an opportunity for Blake to explore one of his favorite themes the world of childhood so memorably delineated in Blake's illuminated book, *Songs of Innocence and Experience*, completed in 1794. Blake was sensitive to the playfulness and enthusiasm of children, but he was also acutely aware of childhood as a transitional state. In this richly suggestive painting we have a profound meditation on the state of childhood, and an intimation of what lies beyond the limits of childish vision.

In spirit the composition, and most of all the technique, is closest to the works of early Italian painting. From the 1770s British collectors and patrons had begun to consider and acquire early Italian paintings. Blake's friend and supporter, the sculptor John Flaxman, had spent a great deal of time on his Grand Tour drawing thirteenth and fourteenth century sculpture, paintings and frescos, consistently praising the qualities of simplicity and grandeur in early Italian art.[10] In Italy Flaxman had met the young artist William Young Ottley who made a series of drawings of early Italian paintings which he would eventually publish in 1826 but which must have been known to Flaxman and Blake. The linearity of *The Virgin Hushing the Young John the Baptist*, the bold mass of the Virgin, the simplicity and grandeur of her drapery and emphatic gesture accord with the strength of design Flaxman and Ottley discovered in the works of early Italian painting. As David Bindman has suggested it may well be that in Blake's so-called tempera works, Blake was 'concerned with finding a way of preserving the linear clarity of watercolor without losing the density of oil painting.'[11]

William Blake *The Nativity, 1799–1800*
Tempera on copper · 10¾ × 15⅛ inches · 273 × 383 mm
Philadelphia Museum of Art: Gift of
Mrs William Thomas Tonner, 1964

William Blake *The Circumcision, 1799–1800*
Tempera on canvas · 10⅛ × 14⅜ inches · 257 × 364 mm
Signed with monogram, lower left
© The Fitzwilliam Museum, Cambridge

Blake's decision to use tempera rather than oil to execute these works also perhaps reflects his interest in early Italian painting; Blake after all referred to the technique as 'fresco'. We have a very detailed explication of the process given by the engraver and antiquarian, J.T. Smith:
Blake's modes for preparing his ground, and laying them over his panels for painting, mixing his colours, and manner of working, were those which he considered to have been practiced by the earliest fresco-painters, whose productions still remain, in numerous instances, vivid and permanently fresh. His ground was a mixture of whiting and carpenter's glue, which he passed over several times in thin coatings: his colours he ground himself, and also united them with the same sort of glue, but in a much weaker state. He would, in the course of painting a picture, pass a very thin transparent wash of glue-water over the whole of the parts he had worked upon, and then proceed to pass a very thin transparent wash of glue-water over the whole of the parts he had worked upon, and then proceed with his finishing.[12]

Although Blake never visited Italy he must have been aware of the fresco fragments which entered British collections during the eighteenth century.[13] Sadly the result of Blake's experimental technique is that his works for Butts tend not to be very stable. A survey of the six tempera paintings by William Blake that still remain in private hands shows that they have mostly severe condition problems.[14] *The Virgin Hushing the Young John the Baptist* is painted on a paper support which has been laid down on fine canvas and is, as a result, by far the best preserved of the group. It is also singular in the group for the strength of its palette, the bold red drapery and clarity of the colouration.

We do not know whether the Butts series was intended to be part of an architectural scheme – Gilchrist merely comments that Butts's house: 'in Fitzroy

Square became a perfect Blake Gallery' – but the paintings might have been arranged typologically, with New Testament scenes paired with episodes in the Old Testament. However, the surviving paintings in the series that deal with Christ's infancy all depict in one way or another on the role of John the Baptist, suggesting that Blake was exploring the life of the Baptist at the same time. The first in the sequence is *The Angel Gabriel appearing to Zacharias* (Metropolitan Museum of Art, New York), which shows the High Priest Zacharias receiving word of the impending birth of his son, John the Baptist. This is followed by the *Nativity* (Philadelphia Museum of Art) in which the Christ Child leaps from the Virgin Mary's body into the hands of John the Baptist's mother, St. Elizabeth. Very unusually, the scene is witnessed by the infant John the Baptist on St. Elizabeth's knee. The precise position of *The Virgin Hushing the Young John the Baptist* in the sequence is not certain – it might follow the *Adoration of the Kings* (Brighton City Art Gallery) and *The Circumcision* (Fitzwilliam Museum, Cambridge) – but it refers back to the Old Testament through John the Baptist, the son of a High Priest, and forward to Christ's sacrifice and the redemption of mankind.[15] The iconographical eccentricities are matched by the boldness of design and exquisite execution which make *The Virgin Hushing the Young John the Baptist* one of the most impressive of the Butts series.

The Butts collection was partly dispersed at auction in 1853, the majority of works having been sold by the beginning of the twentieth century. By 1880 the present painting was in the collection of Edward William Hooper in Cambridge, Massachusetts, who was a very significant figure in the history of Harvard, where he served as Steward from 1872 and Treasurer from 1876. He was evidently closely involved in the arts in the wider Boston area and served as one of the founding trustees of the Museum of Fine Arts in Boston. He was also a considerable collector of Blake's works, his daughters eventually donating to the Houghton Library at Harvard Copy D of Blake's *Jerusalem. The Virgin Hushing the Young John the Baptist* was therefore one of the earliest works by Blake to enter an American collection and has remained in private collections in the US ever since.

This highly impressive, concentrated work is an exceptional distillation of Blake's vision as both a poet and painter. In the Butts commission, Blake was offered the freedom to explore Biblical scenes with his unique imagination. In the present work he produced an outstanding image of motherly love and childhood innocence, inflected by the wider concerns of the Passion and Christ's sacrifice. The playful and innovative addition of the butterfly points to Blake's poetical reading of traditional iconography. Stylistically the canvas shows Blake's profound interest in early Italian painting, the grandeur of the Virgin and bold mass of the red drapery all point to his knowledge of early Florentine frescos. Something also represented by the innovative technique Blake explored. In its preservation, imaginative conceptulisation and beauty, this small picture is one of the most significant works by Blake to come on the market in recent years.

NOTES

1   Alexander Gilchrist, *Life of Blake*, London, 1863, I p.114–115.
2   Martin Butlin, *The Paintings and Drawings of William Blake*, New Haven and London, 1981, I, pp.335–336.
3   Martin Butlin, *The Paintings and Drawings of William Blake*, New Haven and London, 1981, I, p.316.
4   Ed. Geeoffrey Keynes, *The Letters of William Blake, with Related Documents*, Oxford, 1980, p.11.
5   David Bindman, *Blake as an Artist*, Oxford 1977, pp.122–123.
6   Martin Butlin, *The Paintings and Drawings of William Blake*, New Haven and London, 1981, I, no.410, p.328.
7   Ruth Rubinstein, *Michelangelo's lost Sleeping Cupid*, in: *Journal of the Warburg and Courtauld Institutes*, 1986, pp.257–59.
8   David Bindman, *Blake as an Artist*, Oxford 1977, p.116.
9   From a poem by Ippolito Pindemonte on Canova's *Psyche. The Works of Antonio Canova, Engraved in outline by Henry Moses*, London 1824, vol.I, no pagination.
10 Flaxman's Italian journal in the Fitzwilliam Museum, Cambridge, f.18r, reproduced in: eds. Hugh Brigstocke, Eckart Marchand and A.E. Wright, 'John Flaxman and William Young Ottley in Italy', *Walpole Society*, 2010, 72, p.98.
11 David Bindman, *Blake as an Artist*, Oxford 1977, p.117.
12 J.T. Smith, *Nollekens and His Time*, London, 1828, II, p.487.
13 Charles Townley for example, owned a number of fresco fragments by the fourteenth-century painter Spinello Aretino which would have been visible in his house at 7 Park Street. They are now in the National Gallery.
14 See Martin, *The Paintings and Drawings of William Blake*, New Haven and London, 1981, I, cat. nos 396, 398, 416, 417, 671.
15 For a more detailed discussion of these works see David Bindman, David Bindman, *Blake as an Artist*, Oxford 1977, pp.121–23, and Martin, *The Paintings and Drawings of William Blake*, New Haven and London, I, pp.324–29.

THOMAS GIRTIN 1775–1802

Wetherby Bridge and Mills, Yorkshire, looking across the weir

Watercolour over pencil
12½ × 20½ inches · 318 by 521 mm
Painted *c.*1800

COLLECTIONS
Francis W. Keen;
C.A. Keen;
Keen sale, Sotheby's, 20 April 1972, lot 57;
Edward Fremantle, 1984;
Robert Tear, acquired 1984, to 2011;
And by descent, 2014.

LITERATURE
David Hill, *Thomas Girtin, Genius in the North,* exh.cat., Yorkshire (Harewood House), 1999, p.42, no.23;
Greg Smith (ed.), *Thomas Girtin: The Art of Watercolour,* exh.cat., London (Tate), 2002, p.172.

EXHIBITED
Leeds, Harewood House, *Thomas Girtin, Genius in the North,* 1999, no.23;
London, Tate Britain, *Thomas Girtin: The Art of Watercolour,* 2002, no.133.

Henry Edridge
Thomas Girtin sketching at Bushey, 1801
Pencil, with grey wash
4⅜ × 2⅛ inches · 111 × 55 mm
Inscribed: "Girtin" and in another hand "[?] Hearne"
© The Trustees of the British Museum

Writing after the untimely death of Thomas Girtin in 1802, W. H. Pyne, an early chronicler of the development of British watercolour painting observed:

[Girtin's] views of many of our cities, towns, castles, cathedrals, etc, were treated by his pencil in a manner entirely his own; a depth of shadow a brilliancy of light, and a magical splendour of colours characterised his drawings, and displayed a vigour of inherent genius that promised to raise the art [of watercolour] to the highest summit of excellence.[1]

Pyne communicates something of the tonal brilliance of Girtin's work which still marks it out as singular. Girtin was born the same year as Turner and followed a similar early trajectory. Both artists worked in the informal 'academy' established by the amateur artist and physician Dr Thomas Monro – their work from this period often being nearly indistinguishable. Whilst working with Monro Girtin was exposed to the work of John Robert Cozens who was celebrated for producing watercolours where mood and form were the central narrative element. It was this quality which Girtin developed in his own mature works, eschewing simple topography, he imbued his landscape watercolours with a power, dignity and solemnity which pointed to the new possibilities of the medium; his greatest works suggest an emotional response to landscape which is parallel to, but distinct from, that of Turner. Our watercolour executed on a typically panoramic format belongs to the short period of Girtin's maturity dating from early 1799 to his early death at the age of twenty-seven in 1802.

The present watercolour owes something to Cozens in its depth of tone, but Girtin's colouring is more sonorous than Cozens, something which has been attributed to his interest in Flemish landscape.[2] By the date of the present watercolour Girtin had rejected the prevailing approach to watercolour of transparent washes over pencil lines in favour of rich surface effects. His sombre colouring suggests a desire to rival oil painting, to achieve the same kind of depth and mellowness of varnished oil paints with translucent watercolours.

Depicting the bridge at Wetherby on the river Wharfe, Girtin's view dates from one of the trips to Yorkshire he made from 1796. Girtin's had a number of patrons in the north of England including Edward Lascelles of Harewood House who purchased a number of local views and hoped to promote Girtin over Turner in the

elections for the Royal Academy in 1799.[3] The same year Girtin painted the bridge at Harewood which was only a few miles upstream of Wetherby confirming his interest in the picturesque qualities of the stone bridges on the Wharfe. The survival of a pencil study for this view formerly in the collection of Edward Lascelles may suggest that Girtin was planning to sell the finished watercolour to his most consistent Yorkshire patron.[4]

Wetherby was not a popular destination for artists – although Turner did sketch there in 1816 – but Girtin seemed to have understood its picturesque potential. At this date the bridge carried the Great North Road across the river, and the town was an important market and posting centre and some of the inn buildings can be made out beyond the mills. The present view looks from the south bank of the river across the weir to Wetherby mills and bridge. In the present watercolour Girtin has shown work being carried out to the weir in front of the bridge with three figures working to repair damage on the weir where a cart and spade are also visible. David Hill has suggested that this was the result of the heavy flooding which occurred in the winter of 1799 and this would accord with a dating of this watercolour on stylistic grounds to 1800.[5] Another view of the bridge which survives in two versions. A more dramatic treatment of the bridge is in the British Museum, it shows a view looking east, perhaps from the weir, through the bridge's arches towards more cottages and a mill.

Although Girtin's use of unstable indigo pigment has resulted in a change of the overall colour balance – the grey of the sky, depth of shadows and water have been effected – this sheet retains a harmonious beauty whilst demonstrating a breadth and ambition that are testament to its importance to Girtin during the very short period of his artistic maturity. A detailed pencil study survives in the Bacon collection, although Girtin seems unusually not to have made any repetitions.[6]

The present watercolour was first recorded in the collection of Francis W. Keen, a director of Guest, Keen & Nettlefold, who was a significant collector of British watercolours and also owned Girtin's *Morpeth Bridge* now in the Laing Art Gallery.

NOTES

1 W. H. Pyne, 'Observations on the Rise and Progress of Painting in Water Colours', *Repository of Arts*, November 1812-March 1813.

2 Thomas Girtin and David Loshak, *The Art of Thomas* Girtin, London, 1954, p.88.

3 Susan Morris, 'Thomas Girtin', in ed. David Hill, *Thomas Girtin, Genius in the North,* exh. cat., Yorkshire (Harewood House), 1999, P.13.

4 ed. David Hill, *Thomas Girtin, Genius in the North,* exh.cat., Yorkshire (Harewood House), 1999, pp.42–43.

5 ed. David Hill, *Thomas Girtin, Genius in the North,* exh.cat., Yorkshire (Harewood House), 1999, pp.42–43.

6 Thomas Girtin and David Loshak, *The Art of Thomas* Girtin, London, 1954, Cat. no.348, p.182. The subject-matter is misidentified as Hexham Bridge.

Thomas Girtin
Wetherby Bridge, Yorkshire, 1800
Watercolour
12⅝ × 20½ inches · 320 × 521 mm
© The Trustees of the British Museum

JOHN CRANCH 1751–1821

Interior of a Dovecote

Oil on panel
11½ × 10⅛ inches · 290 × 257 mm
Signed 'J. Cranch' (lower right)
Painted *c*.1800

This charming interior view of a dovecote is by John Cranch, a little known but fascinating painter who is best remembered for his contact with the young John Constable. The lamp-lit interior shows Cranch's interest in Dutch painters, such as Teniers and his fascination with the activities of rural life. Cranch's naturalism and interest in subjects beyond the normal range of academic history painting had an important early impact on the young John Constable, who met him with J.T. Smith at Edmonton in 1796. It was this meeting which convinced the young Constable to pursue a career as a painter and Cranch's guidance, both practical and theoretical, had a profound influence on Constable's development as an artist.

Cranch was born at Kingsbridge, Devon, on 12 October 1751. Little is known of his life prior to the exhibition of his first painting at the Society of Artists in 1791, Burning of the Albion Mill, when his address was given as 1 Old Broad Street, London.[1] It seems that Cranch was largely self-taught, although he may have received some instruction from a Catholic priest while a clerk at Axminster. Cranch preferred rural genre themes, exemplified by *Monks with a Lantern in a Moonlit Landscape* of about 1795 and now in the Louvre, Paris, which recalls the lighting effects of Joseph Wright of Derby.[2] Cranch was a close friend of the engraver, draughtsman and drawing master John Thomas

Smith, and the two men played an influential role in the development of the young John Constable.

Constable met Smith and Cranch when engaged on family business outside London – staying with his uncle Thomas Allen, a brewer – the two professional artists offered practical instruction which helped Constable improve his drawing skills, whilst Cranch encouraged his reading. Two of Constable's earliest experiments in oil painting, *The Alchymist* and *The Chymist*, show his stylistic debt to Cranch's interior scenes; Constable himself described his early landscape, *Moonlight Landscape with Hadleigh Church*, in a letter to J.T. Smith: 'I have lately painted a small moonlight in the manner or style of Cranch.'[3] Cranch's importance to the young Constable is demonstrated by the survival of a remarkable document, a memorandum entitled: 'Painter's Reading, and hint or two respecting study.' This engaging list of publications was prepared by Cranch for the young Constable in September 1796 and includes a survey of literature for the aspiring painter. Cranch notes that Reynolds's *Discourses* should be read with caution, as 'they go' he explains: 'to establish an aristocracy in painting:

they betray, and I believe have betrayed, many students into a contempt of everything but grandeur and Michael Angelo: the force, and the splendid eloquence, with which the precepts are inculcated, makes us forget, that the truth of Teniers, and the wit and moral purpose of Hogarth, have been, and will for ever be at least as useful, and diffuse at least much pleasure, as the mere sublimities of Julio and Raphael.[4]

For Cranch Reynolds's hierarchy of painting was too restrictive, so he advised the young Constable to study: 'the general

habitudes of men and things; or Nature, as she is more and less perverted by the social institutions.' This cry for naturalism was one that Constable would echo throughout his career and seek to emulate.

Cranch exhibited only nine paintings during his lifetime, seven of which were shown at the 1808 British Institution exhibition. Cranch also published two treatises: On the Economy of Testaments in 1794, and Inducements to promote the fine arts of Great Britain by exciting native genius to independent effort and original design in 1811. This rare panel of two figures in a *Dovecote* perfectly illustrates his style and the aspects of his painting which most appealed to the young Constable.

John Cranch *Plasterer, 1807*
Oil on panel ᵃ 5¾ × 6¼ inches · 146 × 159 mm
Signed
Yale Center for British Art, Paul Mellon Collection

John Thomas Smith
John Cranch, 1795
Stipple, etching and engraving
8⅞ × 7 inches · 225 × 177 mm
© The Trustees of the British Museum

NOTES

1 For Cranch's works see ed. Hugh Belsey, *From Gainsborough to Constable; the emergence of naturalism in British Landscape Painting 1750–1810*, exh.cat. Sudbury (Gainsborough's House), 1991, pp.58–62.

2 Eds. Élisabeth Foucart-Walter, Olivier Meslay and Dominique Thiébaut, *Catalogue des peintures britanniques, espagnoles, germaniques, scandinaves et diverses du musée du Louvre*, Paris, 2013, no.R.F.1991–17, p.22.

3 Graham Reynolds, *The Early Paintings and Drawings of John Constable*, New Haven and London, 1996, no.96.1 p.7.

4 eds. Leslie Parish, Conal Shields and Ian Fleming-Williams, *John Constable: Further Documents & Correspondence*, London, 1975, pp.199–201.

JAMES WARD RA 1769–1859

Sunset

Pencil and watercolour heightened with
gouache and gum arabic
7⅛ × 10 inches · 181 × 254 mm
Signed with initials 'JWRA' (lower right)

COLLECTIONS
Private collection, 1982;
Anthony Spink, 1999;
Private collection, USA, 2014.

LITERATURE
Oliver Beckett, *The Life and Work of James
Ward RA 1769–1859 The Forgotten Genius,*
Lewes, 1995, repr. opposite p.195;
Lowell Libson (ed.), *Feeling Through the Eye,*
exh.cat., 2000, pp.46 & 100.

EXHIBITED
London, Spink-Leger, *Feeling Through the Eye,*
2000, no.106.

Oliver Beckett noted that the present
drawing by James Ward is:
*… brushed in with enormous confidence
and freedom, it exemplifies his mastery of a
medium made their own by the distinguished
circle of British water-colourists to whose
genius Ward has paid such an eloquent tribute.*[1]

James Ward was a remarkably prolific
and wide ranging artist, producing grand
historical canvases as well as intimate,
observational sketches. A free sketch of a
sunset worked over in watercolour, with
gouache and gum arabic, this drawing is
a rare example of James Ward's landscape
colour studies. Not easily datable, this
sheet seems unlikely to have been made
in preparation for a larger composition
– although sunsets form an important
component in a number of Ward's grand
exhibition works – instead it represents
a powerfully immediate response to an
actual landscape. This immediacy places
Ward's drawing in the context of the
explosion of *plein air* painting in European
art around 1800.

Ward's earliest paintings were dominated by the influence of George Morland, his
brother-in-law although it was Peter Paul
Rubens had the more lasting impact. As
William Carey noted in 1809, Ward's paintings were: 'Not the School of Morland
– but the resurrection of Rubens.'[2] It
is Rubens, and particularly Rubens the
landscape painter, who inflects much of
Ward's most celebrated work. But Ward's
interest in imitation did not prevent his
fascination with drawing from nature. As
several writers have observed, his earliest
works show the impact of Thomas Girtin
and it was assumed that he was a member

of Girtin's sketching society known as 'the brothers' although there is no proof that he ever worked with Girtin. Ward was member of another sketching society, one largely overlooked in the literature. In March 1804 Ward reported to Farington that:

He & 5 other Artists…have for four years past been accustomed to meet once a week during the winter Season at each others Houses alternately, to sketch and converse upon Art.[3]

This group is of particular interest as four of the six – Samuel Shelley, John Claude Nattes, Robert Hills and Henry Pyne – formed the Society of Painters in Water-colours the same year to give an alternative exhibition space in London for artists working in watercolour. Although they seem not to have painted *en plein air*, Ward frequently went on sketching trips with Robert Hills and both produced powerful on the spot landscape drawings. At the same moment in Rome a group of pensionnaires at the Académie de France à Rome were painting immediate studies from nature in the Italian landscape, artists such as Simon Denis, Pierre-Henri Valenciennes and François-Marius Granet. Ward's bold, liquid drawing which captures in a few elemental brushstrokes both the visual sensation and feeling of a sunset is perfectly in tune with the studies being made in Rome.

The boldly handled sheet demonstrates both Ward's facility as technician in water-colour and his ability to exploit the medium to create a work charged with energy and emotion. The romantic outlook is combined with a search for realistic truth; the careful pencil marks show Ward's attempt to record the sky accurately. But ultimately Ward's drawn details are submerged and embodied in his large and poetic generalisation. Like

Simon Denis (1755–1813)
Sunset, Rome, c.1789–1806
Oil on paper · 8¼ × 10⅜ inches · 210 × 264 mm
Thaw Collection, Jointly Owned by The Metropolitan Museum of Art and The Morgan Library & Museum, Gift of Eugene V. Thaw, 2009

his contemporaries working in Rome, sunsets feature prominently in Ward's work – he places one in the background of his portrait of Napoleon's horse *Marengo* painted in 1824 – sunsets were both spectacular and poetically suggestive. Despite the diminutive scale of the sheet Ward is here as romantic as any of his larger exhibition machines.

NOTES

1   Oliver Beckett, *The Life and Work of James Ward RA 1769–1859: The Forgotten Genius*, Lewes, 1995, coloured plates opposite p.195.

2   William Carey, *Letter to I*** A*****, Esq., A Connoisseur in London*, Manchester, 1809, p.11.

3   Ed. Kenneth Garlick and Angus Macintyre, *The Diary of Joseph Farington*, New Haven and London, 1979, VI, p.2271.

SIR THOMAS LAWRENCE PRA 1769–1830

The Wellesley-Pole Sisters

left: Lady Mary
(wife of Sir Charles Bagot)

centre: Lady Emily
(wife of Lord FitzRoy Somerset, 1st
Baron Raglan)

right: Lady Priscilla
(wife of John, Lord Burghersh, 11th Earl
of Westmorland)

Pencil, black and red chalk and pink
wash on paper, watermark 'J Whatman
1810'
18⅞ × 15⅛ inches · 480 × 384 mm
Signed and dated 'T Lawrence 1814'
(lower left) and also signed with initials
and dated 'T.L. 1814' (lower right)

COLLECTIONS
Lady Emily Wellesley-Pole, one of the sitters;
Richard, 2nd Baron Raglan,
son of the above, 1884;
George, 3rd Baron Raglan, 1921;
Fitzroy, 4th Baron Raglan, 1964;
Fitzroy, 5th Baron Raglan, 2010;
and by descent, to 2014.

LITERATURE
George Somes Layard, *Sir Thomas Lawrence's
Letter-Bag*, London, 1906, reproduced,
opposite p.103;
John Steegman, *Portraits in Welsh Houses*,
Cardiff, 1962, vol.II, no.32, p.129;
Kenneth Garlick, 'A catalogue of the paint-
ings, drawings and pastels of Sir Thomas
Lawrence', *The Walpole Society*, XXXIX,
London, 1963, pp. 218–219;
Michael Levey, *Sir Thomas Lawrence 1769–1830*,
exh.cat., 1979, p.104;
Michael Levey, *Sir Thomas Lawrence,* New
Haven and London, 2005, p.4, repr. on p.6;
Cassandra Albinson, Peter Funnell and
Lucy Peltz (eds.), *Thomas Lawrence: Regency
Power & Brilliance*, exh.cat., New Haven and
London, p.131.

EXHIBITED
Cwmbran, Llantarnam Grange Arts Centre,
Portraits from Monmouthshire Houses, 1977,
no.18;
London, National Portrait Gallery, *Sir
Thomas Lawrence*, 1979–1980, no.77.

ENGRAVED
By James Thomson, published Oct. 1. 1827 by
Moon, Boys & Graves;
By J.B. Longacre as 'The Three Sisters'.

*… Lawrence has fortunately left a mass of
evidence of his skill in drawing upon paper – and
with it some surprises. As well as single, at one
precise and lightly finished portrait drawings
in chalk, he could produce occasional group
portraits, seldom more ambitiously accomplished
than in the trio of Lord Mornington's daughters,
casually yet elegantly seated on the ground, a
group of contemporary Graces. The idiom of
the composition is naturalistic, with emphasis
strongest on the individual features of the three
sisters, but in its overall concept, as in the group-
ing and the delicate play of line, there seems some
hovering influence of Flaxman.*
MICHAEL LEVEY [1]

Lawrence's 1814 portrait of the nieces of
the Duke of Wellington, *The Wellesley-Pole
Sisters*, stands as one of the finest finished
drawings of his maturity. Compositionally
a highly sophisticated mediation of classical
and Renaissance models, this delicate and
highly finished work demonstrates the full
weight of Lawrence's sophistication as a
draughtsman. Yet meticulously observed
and complexly arranged portrait drawings
such as this raise certain questions about
Lawrence's technique and the status of
finished drawings at this key moment in
his career.

A child prodigy, Thomas Lawrence was
self-trained as a draughtsman and drew small
portraits in pastels in Bath for three guineas
each before moving to London in 1787. He
attended the Royal Academy Schools briefly
but pressure from commissions forced
him to leave. He continued to produce
and exhibit spectacular finished drawings,
including the highly wrought portrait of
Mary Hamilton (British Museum) which
was exhibited at the Academy in 1789. After

Sir Thomas Lawrence
Mary Hamilton
Pencil and red and black chalk · 18 × 12¼ inches · 458 × 312 mm
Signed with monogram *TL* and dated 1789
© The Trustees of the British Museum

initial success on the walls of the Royal Academy, Lawrence became a full member of the Academy in 1794 at the age of 25 and by 1800 was considered the leading portrait painter in Britain. The ensuing decade saw him consolidate his position so that by 1814 he was at the height of his powers as a painter and on the eve of the most productive period of his career. With the Duke of Wellington's victory at Waterloo and the conclusion of the Napoleonic Wars, the Prince Regent commissioned Lawrence to complete a series of full-length portraits of the victorious allied commanders. The portrait of the *The Wellesley-Pole Sisters* was drawn on the eve of the victory at Waterloo and perfectly demonstrates Lawrence's compositional and technical sophistication. The choice of medium is perhaps less explicable, as by 1814 he had all but abandoned large-scale portrait drawings of this kind. Lawrence's choice therefore demands some elucidation.

The sitters were Charlotte Anne, Emily Harriet and Priscilla Anne Wellesley-Pole, the daughters of William, 3rd Earl of Mornington, the Duke of Wellington's eldest brother. The immediate impetus for the commission seems to have been the marriage in August 1814 of Emily Harriet to Lord Fitzroy Somerset. The present portrait seems likely to have been commissioned on the eve of Emily Harriet's marriage as a memento of her siblings. Lawrence completed a portrait of Lady Emily in 1814 which he exhibited at the Royal Academy the same year and which is now in the Hermitage, St Petersburg. The commission of an intimate drawing of all three siblings was possibly prompted – if not initiated – by the Duke of Wellington himself.

Fitzroy Somerset was the Duke of Wellington's military secretary and close confidante and the three sisters were all close to their uncle, with whom they were all staying in Paris later in 1814. Lawrence had already at this date painted a portrait of the Duke and more pertinently drawn an engaging portrait of his wife, Catherine Duchess of Wellington, for her sister, Mrs Henry Hamilton.[2] As will be seen Wellington was conscious of Lawrence's position as the pre-eminent artist in Britain and the importance of promoting British painting in the wake of Napoleon's fall. Perhaps most compelling is the survival of a receipt in the archives at Stratfield Saye from Mary Smirke dated 25 May 1818 for a copy of the present drawing. Mary Smirke, the daughter of the painter Robert Smirke, was employed by Lawrence as a professional copyist, Wellington therefore owned a copy of the drawing which remains with his descendants at Stratfield Saye.[3] This would suggest that the original drawing was at the very least admired by the duke, if not directly commissioned by him as a gift for Lady Fitzroy Somerset.

Shortly after the portrait was completed – October 1814 – Lawrence was corresponding with one of the sitters, Priscilla, Lady Burghesh, who was then in Paris staying with Wellington. Lady Burghesh wrote to Lawrence noting: 'I have not failed to mention to Ld. Wellington your desire of shewing the French your painting of Rolla, and he will be delighted to have a fine production of English art seen in his house, if its dimensions… will allow of its being placed there', adding: 'the Duke and I have fixed upon his dining-room as the best calculated to contain it, and he would admit all persons to see it… I have seen Mr.

Michelangelo (1475–1564)
Doni Tondo, c.1507
Oil and tempera on panel
47½ inches · 1200 mm diam
The Uffizi Gallery, Florence

Sir Thomas Lawrence
Mrs Isabella Wolff, 1815
Oil on canvas
50½ × 40¼ inches · 1282 × 1023 mm
Art Institute of Chicago

William Lock, who highly approves of your showing French artists that correctness of drawing is not exclusively their own.'[4] The portrait being referred to was Lawrence's full-length portrait of the actor *John Philip Kemble as Coriolanus* which had been exhibited at the Royal Academy in 1800. In a letter dated June 1816, the Duke of Wellington confirmed the offer adding: 'I will take care they [Lawrence's paintings] shall be plac'd in a situation to do them Justice and to convince even the vain Parisians of the superiority of our English Artist.'[5] The idea that Lawrence – or his supporters, Lady Burghesh and his friend and patron William Lock II of Norbury – were concerned with demonstrating to French artists the 'correctness of drawing' is suggestive. Whilst 'drawing' here referred to painting, it could well be that Lawrence was aware of the drawings of artists such as Jean-Auguste-Dominique Ingres, then living in Rome and producing finely rendered and carefully composed group portraits of British sitters in Rome. The stark modernity of Ingres's drawn portraits may well have prompted Lawrence to reconsider the medium.

Turning to the drawing itself, it is clear to see Lawrence's immediate visual stimulus was his own collection of old master drawings. The arrangement of Lady Emily Anne – kneeling, seated on her legs, her left hand holding her left foot – recalls the Virgin in Michelangelo's *Doni Tondo* seen in reverse. Whilst the motif of the kneeling figure closely recalls Michelangelo, so too the arrangements of the three heads recall the relationship of the Holy Family. It was at precisely this moment that Lawrence was most keenly

James Thomson (after Sir Thomas Lawrence)
The Three Sisters
Stipple engraving
23¾ × 18 inches · 605 × 459 mm
published Oct. 1. 1827 by Moon, Boys & Graves
© The Trustees of the British Museum

interested in the works of Michelangelo. He was particularly keen to explore the potential for some of Michelangelo's more complex poses in his own female portraiture. In 1815 Lawrence finished his remarkable portrait of *Isabella Wolff* now in the Art Institute of Chicago. The sitter is shown in a pose derived from Michelangelo's *Erythraean Sibyl*, whilst Wolff herself is depicted examining a book of drawings derived from Michelangelo. Whilst in *The Wellesley-Pole sisters* Michelangelo's weight and solemnity has been lightened his linear invention surely lies behind the composition? Michael Levey sensed the 'hovering influence of Flaxman', although it is difficult to read Flaxman's stark linear neo-classicism in such a delicate and complexly articulated drawing; in contrast to the bold actions of Flaxman's figures, the bejewelled, interlocking hands of Lawrence's composition point towards Italian Mannerist precedents.

Lawrence's decision to compose a highly finished drawing may directly reflect Lawrence's awareness of Michelangelo's highly finished presentation drawings. Certainly the decision to produce a drawn portrait, rather than a large oil, reflected an aesthetic decision as much as a commercial or practical one. Lawrence may have felt that three elegant young women, delicately intertwined, lent themselves to a drawing. As Lawrence's most ambitious multi-figure drawing the present sheet certainly occupied a distinct position as opposed to a finished oil.

Several copies and engravings exist of the composition. The same size copy made by Mary Smirke for which the Duke of Wellington paid 40 guineas was the most elaborate. The drawing was engraved by James Thomson in 1827 and again, titled *The Three Sisters*, by J.B. Longacre. A drawing of just the heads of the sitters by a follower of Lawrence survives in the Taft Museum of Art, Cincinnati and Garlick records a number of copies of the individual heads.[6] Elizaveta Renne has challenged the identification of the sitters, suggesting that the figure on the left is in fact Lady Emily Harriet Wellesley-Pole, rather than the central figure.[7] Although it seems likely, given the initial owner of the drawing was Lady Emily Harriet, that she is the central figure and her physiognomy is entirely consistent with Lawrence's oil portrait of her made the same year.[8]

Lawrence's highly sophisticated and exquisitely rendered portrait of *The Wellesley-Pole Sisters* demonstrates his extraordinary ability as a draughtsman. The boldness of conception and skill of execution show Lawrence working at the height of his powers at a moment when he was about to prove himself as one of the most incisive and intelligent portraitists in Europe. Drawing on the work of Michelangelo Lawrence has created an ambitious and complex sheet which, as Michael Levey has suggested, celebrates the sitters as the modern day three graces.

NOTES

1 Michael Levey, *Sir Thomas Lawrence*, New Haven and London, 2005, p.4.

2 The portrait of the Duchess of Wellington is reproduced in: Lord Ronald Sutherland Gower, *Sir Thomas Lawrence*, London, 1900, plate facing p.153.

3 Kenneth Garlick, 'A catalogue of the paintings, drawings and pastels of Sir Thomas Lawrence', *The Walpole Society*, 1962–1964, xxxix, p.219.

4 George Somes Layard, *Sir Thomas Lawrence's Letter-Bag*, London, 1906, p.103. For the original letter: London, Royal Academy Library, LAW/2/83.

5 George Somes Layard, *Sir Thomas Lawrence's Letter-Bag*, London, 1906, p.104.

6 Josephine C. Galbraith, 'Two Drawings by Sir Thomas Lawrence in the Taft Collection', *Bulletin of the Cincinnati Art Museum*, April 1935, VI, 2, pp.40–41.

7 Elizaveta Renne, *State Hermitage Museum Catalogue: Sixteenth to Nineteenth Century British Painting*, New Haven and London, 2011, no.65, pp.132–137.

8 Renne makes several unsustainable assertions about the present drawing, claiming it was drawn in 1811, despite it being dated 1814 and confusing it with Mary Smirke's copy at Stratfield Saye which she reproduces as the original. See Elizaveta Renne, *State Hermitage Museum Catalogue: Sixteenth to Nineteenth Century British Painting*, New Haven and London, 2011, no.65, pp.132–137.

May 25 – 1818

Received of the Duke of Wellington by Sir Thos Lawrence made by him forty Guineas for a the Copy of a Drawing – containing the portraits of The Honble. Mrs Bagot, Lady Burghersh & Lady Fitzroy Somerset

M. Smirke

£42: 0

Receipt £42 from Mary Smirke dated 25 May 1818 for a copy of the present drawing. Transcription: *Received of the Duke of Wellington by Sir Thos Lawrence made by him forty guineas for a the Copy of Drawing – containing the portraits of The Honble. Mrs Bagot, Lady Burghersh, & Lady Fitzroy Somerset M. Smirke £42: 0*
© Stratfield Saye Preservation Trust

SIR GEORGE HOWLAND BEAUMONT BT 1753–1827

The Lake District Tour of 1815: a sketchbook

Pencil and monochrome wash on paper
3⅞ × 5 inches · 97 × 127 mm
Now containing 88 leaves, variously signed
and dated between 1814 and 1815 and some
inscribed
Inscribed on the front cover: 'A Sketch Book
of Sir George Beaumont's The gift of Lady
Beaumont to ASB 1828'

COLLECTIONS
Margaret, Lady Beaumont, the artist's widow;
ASB, a gift from the above in 1828;
Private collection.

This sketchbook records a trip made by the
great patron and amateur painter Sir George
Beaumont from his house Coleorton Hall
in Leicestershire to the Lake District in
1815. Beaumont was one of the outstanding
figures to visit the Lake District, significantly
contributing to its popularity amongst both

John Hoppner (1758 – 1810)
Sir George Beaumont, 1803
Oil on canvas
30½ × 25⅛ inches · 775 × 639 mm
© National Gallery, London,
Bequeathed by Claude Dickason Rotch, 1962

professional painters and amateurs.[1] The
small, pocket-sized sketchbook contains
a number of pencil and wash studies of
landscapes around Borrowdale, Langdale
and Brougham Castle, all made in
September 1815. The studies offer an insight
into Beaumont's working practice, one that
reflected the activities of the painters he
knew and encouraged including Thomas
Hearne, Joseph Farington and particularly
John Constable.

Beaumont was educated at Eton College,
where Alexander Cozens taught him
drawing. This became his passion after a
sketching holiday spent with his tutor, the
Revd Charles Davy, the engraver William
Woollett, and Woollett's apprentice Thomas
Hearne. While at New College, Oxford
Beaumont joined the drawing master John
Baptist Malchair on sketching expeditions.
Through Oxford connections he met
the painters who were to be his lifelong
heroes, the landscapist Richard Wilson and
the portraitist Sir Joshua Reynolds. Both
nurtured his interest in the old masters:
Wilson introduced him to the work of
Claude Lorrain, and in 1792 Reynolds would
bequeath him Sébastien Bourdon's Return
of the Ark, now held by the National Gallery
in London.

Beaumont visited the Lake District
throughout the 1790s forging a close friendship with a number of the Romantic poets
resident in the area; William Wordsworth
would remain a lifelong friend and correspondent. A remarkable drawing by Thomas
Hearne depicting Beaumont and Joseph
Farington sketching the waterfall at Lodore,
Derwentwater, shows Beaumont working
en plein air seated under an umbrella.[2]
Beaumont and Farington returned to the

Lake District on numerous occasions over
the next two decades and it is Farington who
records in December 1816 a conversation with
the painter William Owen which mentions
the context of the present sketchbook:
*Owen told me He had this day recd. a long letter
from Sir George Beaumont with some gain. Sir
George expatiated much on the beauties of the
Scenery of the Lakes where He had lately passed
three months, & He exorted Owen to go to that
delightful Country.*[3]

This almost certainly refers to the trip
on which Beaumont completed the present
sketchbook. Several of the views are annotated allowing us to reconstruct the trip which
took him from Coleorton to Borrowdale,
then south to Little Langdale where he
made a sketch of Beild Crag. Beaumont then
moved east sketching along the Lowther
River and at the ruins of Brougham Castle
close to Penrith before concluding the sketchbook at Barnard Castle. He almost certainly
met the Wordsworths at Grasmere. It was in
1815 that Wordsworth allowed Beaumont to
contribute engravings from his own paintings
to the *Miscellaneous Poems* and *The White Doe*.
The pencil and wash drawings contained in
our sketchbook offer an evocative record of
Beaumont's trip to Cumbria and his love of
'the beauties of the *Scenery of the Lakes.*'

NOTES
1   For Beaumont and the Lake District see John
    Murdoch, *The Discovery of the Lake District: A
    Northern Arcadia and its Uses*, exh.cat., London
    (Victoria and Albert Museum), 1984, pp.20–24.
2   Ed. Jonathan Wordsworth, Michael Jaye and
    Robert Woof, *William Wordsworth and the Age
    of English Romanticism*, Rutgers, 1987, pp.89–92.
3   Ed. Kathryn Cave, *The Diary of Joseph
    Farington*, New Haven and London, 1984, XIV,
    p.4943.

JOHN CONSTABLE RA 1776–1837

Woodland Landscape, Autumn 1815

Oil on millboard
14½ × 24½ inches · 368 × 622 mm
Painted in 1815–16

COLLECTIONS
Private collection to 2010;
Private collection, UK, to 2014.

[fig.1] John Constable
Edge of a Wood, c.1816
Oil on canvas
36¼ × 28⅜ inches · 921 × 721 mm
Art Gallery of Ontario, Toronto
Gift of Reuben Wells Leonard Estate, 1936

This fascinating woodland scene was unknown to Constable scholars until it recently, when it was recognised as being closely related to a similar, albeit smaller and more highly finished painting by the artist, *Edge of a Wood c.*1816 (fig.1).[1] Both pictures seem to show the same stretch of Suffolk woodland, and both include a similar donkey with her foal as well as the same red cloaked figure collecting firewood. They are of particular interest in marking an intriguing moment in Constable's mid career when he had developed a more 'finished' style for his exhibition pictures, sometimes painted in the open air, and – in the case of these two works – also closely imitating the style and character of the work of his predecessor, fellow-Suffolk artist Thomas Gainsborough whose art he greatly admired.

Constable was born in 1776 in the Suffolk village of East Bergholt, son of a prosperous corn and coal merchant, Golding Constable. In 1799 he embarked on his artistic training in London, entering the Royal Academy Schools, and by 1802 had become determined to specialise in landscape rather than the more lucrative or prestigious modes of portraiture or history painting. He also decided to concentrate on the rather unassuming Suffolk scenes he associated with his childhood in and around Dedham Vale, the village of East Bergholt and at Flatford on the river Stour where the family milling business was based. Constable was later to write that it was these scenes which had 'made him a painter'.

Until his marriage and permanent move to London in 1816, Constable would usually spend long summers at his parents' house in East Bergholt, sometimes undertaking local commissions but more often sketching close to home, gathering new material for his exhibition canvases. He sometimes started work on these whilst still in Suffolk (in 1802 his father acquired the lease on a building in the village for Constable's use as a studio) but would then refine and finish them in London over the winter, submitting them to the Academy exhibitions the following spring.

In the winter of 1815–16, however, Constable altered this practice. His mother had died earlier in the year and when in the autumn of 1815 his father also began to show signs of serious ill health, the artist decided to spend the entire winter in East Bergholt, with just the occasional visit to London. Rather than working in his studio on the High Street, it seems likely that Constable would have set up a painting room in the family house during this period so as to be close to his father, and indeed we know that two paintings he made earlier that summer, *Golding Constable's Flower Garden* and *Golding Constable's Kitchen Garden* 1815 (both Ipswich Museum and Art Galleries) were painted by him from rooms at the back of East Bergholt House.[2] It was presumably also here, in a room in the house, that during the winter of 1815–16 Constable worked on the two exhibition canvases he was to send in to the Academy exhibition the following year, *A Wheatfield* and *A Wood: Autumn*.

A Wheatfield, whose whereabouts was unknown to Constable scholars until 1988–9 and is now in the Clark Art Institute of Art in Williamstown, seems largely to have been painted by Constable on the spot during August and early September 1815, although certain elements – such as the figures and highly detailed plants and foliage in the foreground – would surely have been added

[fig.2] John Constable
Study of the Trunk of an Elm Tree. c.1821
Oil on paper
12 × 19¾ inches · 306 × 248 mm
Signed with initials
© Victoria & Albert Museum, London,
Gift of Isabel Constable

by him in his painting room.[3] The identification of *A Wood: Autumn*, meanwhile, was only made as recently as 2005 when *Edge of a Wood* was re-dated to *c*.1815–16 (and very plausibly suggested as the missing 1816 exhibit *A Wood; Autumn*) following the discovery by Jennifer Thompson of an oil study of two donkeys in the Philadelphia Museum of Art dated 29th Feb 1816 (fig.3) closely related to those in the left-hand foregrounds of the Toronto picture and the present work, *Woodland Landscape*.[4]

Constable only rarely painted autumn landscapes. Indeed according to his biographer C. R. Leslie, Constable once placed a violin on a patch of green lawn to demonstrate to his patron Sir George Beaumont that brown autumnal tints were not appropriate (as his traditionally-minded patron believed) for summer landscapes such as Constable himself painted.[5] *Edge of a Wood ('A Wood: Autumn')*, and this related compositional study *Woodland Landscape*, are therefore particularly unusual and indeed seem to be the first fully elaborated autumn subjects that Constable had attempted by this date. They were to be followed by just a handful of other autumnal pictures later in his career, the *Helmingham Dell* subjects of *c*.1826 and 1830, and the *Cenotaph* of 1836 (National Gallery), the latter showing a grove of trees at the Leicestershire residence of Sir George Beaumont.[6]

Why would Constable decide to paint an exhibitable autumn landscape in 1816? The immediate answer is that, untypically, he was in Suffolk throughout the autumn in 1815, and had every opportunity to make sketches outdoors at that time and, given the good weather, there is every evidence that he did so. On 19 October he wrote to his fiancée

Maria Bicknell: 'I have really been every day intending to write to you but I have been so much out, endeavouring to catch the last of this beautifull [*sic*] year, that I have neglected almost every other duty'.[7] Even as late as 3 December he told Maria in another letter that the previous day had been 'so very mild that I went painting in the field from a donkey that I wanted to introduce in a little picture' – some three months, as it happens, before he painted the study of donkeys he was to use in *Edge of a Wood ('A Wood: Autumn')* and in *Woodland Landscape*.[8]

There is, however, another good reason why Constable might have chosen to paint an autumn landscape at this particular juncture in his life. He had always admired the work of fellow landscapist Thomas Gainsborough, and seems at this date still to have favoured the artist's early work based on Dutch masters such as Ruisdael and Hobbema and notable for its careful level of finish.[9] Indeed, there is one particular early landscape by Gainsborough which Constable knew well, the view of *Cornard Wood, near Sudbury, Suffolk* (National Gallery, London; fig.4) which his maternal uncle David Pike Watts had acquired at some stage between 1808 and 1814, and which Constable would often have seen when visiting his uncle at his house in London, at Portland Place.[10] Pike Watts also lent *Cornard Wood* to the British Institution in 1814 for a retrospective exhibition of the work of Gainsborough, Hogarth and Wilson and Zoffany, an exhibition we know Constable visited.[11]

Indeed, it seems that Constable painted his 1816 Academy exhibit, *Edge of a Wood (A Wood; Autumn)*, together with its related compositional study, *A Woodland*, with Gainsborough's *Cornard Wood* uppermost in his mind. Although, as Hugh Belsey points out, commentators neither now or then seem to have highlighted the fact that *Cornard Wood* is an autumn scene, this is of course how viewers – including Pike Watts and Constable himself – would have interpreted it; not only is the foliage distinctly autumnal in colour but the figures busily collecting firewood and sand are surely stocking up on supplies of these materials given winter is fast approaching.

Constable's inclusion of two donkeys at the left of both compositions, even though based on a sketch made from the life, closely echo the two creatures in *Cornard Wood*, whilst the red-cloaked figure gathering firewood similarly echoes a figure tying up a bundle of twigs in Gainsborough's picture on the left. Interestingly, this same rather generalised and archaising red-cloaked figure with black hat appears in Constable's earlier exhibition painting, *A Church Porch, East Bergholt* 1810 (Tate) and seems to have been deployed by him when wishing to invoke associations with eighteenth-century literature or artistic prototypes.[12] Its inclusion in these two autumn woodland landscapes may similarly indicate that Constable wished them to be read as paying homage to eighteenth-century representations of these scenes (and via those, to earlier Dutch prototypes) and specifically to Gainsborough's *Cornard Wood*.

Indeed Constable may even have been hoping to flatter his uncle by directly imitating this, one of the most prized paintings in his collection, and to prove to him (in the light of his uncle's complaints on this issue) that he was capable of producing a picture with as much careful 'finish' as his predecessor. He was also well aware that Pike Watts, like Beaumont, favoured pictures presented under what his uncle termed 'the admired October

tints'.[13] If so, the gamble paid off, as Pike Watts decided to purchase Constable's *Wood: Autumn* from the 1816 Academy exhibition.[14]

It has been suggested that the stretch of woodland shown in *Edge of a Wood (A Wood: Autumn),* and thus also in *A Woodland Landscape*, might be somewhere in Helmingham Park just outside Ipswich, the seat of Constable's patrons the Earls of Dysart (the Tollemache family). Certainly Constable had sketched there when a young man, and was to produce a number of paintings of *Helmingham Dell* in later years based on an important early drawing made in the park.[15] However, there is no record that he visited Helmingham around this date, nor did he have any outstanding commissions with the Tollemache family which might have necessitated a visit there at this time. Indeed, given his desire to stay close to his ailing father, it seems just as likely that the woods shown in these two paintings were local to East Bergholt.

Unlike *The Wheatfield*, however, these two woodland scenes were probably painted by Constable chiefly indoors. *Woodland Landscape* is painted on millboard and also has extensive pinholes around its edges, both of which features – were it to have been painted before 1816 – would tend to point to *plein-air* work but which by 1816 are less conclusive indicators.[16] Indoors or outdoors, *plein-air* or studio work, both paintings nevertheless reveal the careful attention paid to 'finishing' which one associates with Constable's style in the period 1814–17, refined through outdoor work and direct observation but also strongly mediated through Gainsborough.

ANNE LYLES

[fig.3] John Constable
Two Donkeys, 1816
Oil on canvas mounted on panel
7½ × 9⅞ inches · 149 × 200 mm
Philadelphia Museum of Art: John G. Johnson Collection, 1917

[fig.4] Thomas Gainsborough
Cornard Wood, near Sudbury, Suffolk, 1748
Oil on canvas
48 × 61 inches · 1220 × 1550 mm
© The National Gallery, London Bought (Lewis Fund), 1875
Inventory number NG925

NOTES

1　Graham Reynolds, *The Early Paintings and Drawings of John Constable*, New Haven and London, 1996, no.02.1, where dated 1802 following article by David G. Taylor, 'New Light on an Early Painting by John Constable', *Burlington Magazine*, CXXII, Aug 1980, pp.566–68; but now redated to 1815–16 and identified as Reynolds 16.2 (see note 4)

2　Reynolds, op.cit, nos 15.23 and 15.24.

3　Reynolds, *ibid*, no.16.1 (Clark Art Institute 2007.8.27).

4　Jennifer A. Thompson, 'A rediscovered oil sketch by John Constable', *Burlington Magazine*, CXLVII, Sept 2005, pp.608–12. In fact Sarah Cove had always doubted Taylor's dating of *Edge of a Wood* to 1802, as its ground, priming and use of Mars colours are all incompatible with Constable's early work, and she similarly proposed it as the artist's missing Academy exhibit of 1816 (S. Cove, 'Very Great Difficulty in Composition and Execution: the Materials and Techniques of Constable's sky and cloud studies of the 1820s' in F. Bancroft ed, *Constable's Skies*, Salander O'Reilly Galleries, exh cat., New York, 2004, p.139.

5　C.R.Leslie, *Memoirs of the Life of John Constable*, first pub. 1843; see 1951 edition (ed J. Mayne), p.114.

6　Graham Reynolds, *The Later Paintings and Drawings of John Constable*, New Haven and London, 1984, nos.26.21, 30.1, 30.2 and 30.3 (all versions of *Helmingham Dell*) and 36.1 (*The Cenotaph*).

7　R.B.Beckett ed, *John Constable's Correspondence: Early Friends and Maria Bicknell (Mrs Constable)*, Ipswich 1964, II, p.156.

8　*Ibid*, p.162. For another study of a donkey painted by Constable around this time, dated 27 Feb 1816, see Christie's, 7 July 2010, lot 171.

9　In 1799, when only 23 years old, Constable told Farington he thought 'first pictures of Gainsborough his best, latter so wide of nature'. However, by the time he gave his Lectures on Landscape Painting in 1836 and spoke of the ability of Gainsborough's paintings to 'bring tears in our eyes' it is clear he was responding to the emotional appeal of the artist's later work.

10　Pike Watts may have acquired *Cornard Wood* directly from Josiah Boydell in 1808. We know it was certainly in his collection by 1814 as he lent it that year to the British Institution (J. Egerton, *National Gallery Catalogues: the British School*, London 1998, p.72).

11　A letter from Constable to Maria Constable of 22 June 1814 refers to his visiting the British Institution to see this exhibition, which he had earlier told her (letter 4 May) he was eagerly anticipating (R.B.Beckett, 1964, pp.126 and 122).

12　For *A Church Porch, East Bergholt* (exh RA 1810), see Reynolds 1996, no.10.2 and L. Parris, *The Tate Gallery Constable Collection*, London, 1981, p.50, where he links the painting to the tradition of churchyard melancholy in painting and poetry going back to Thomas Gray's famous *Elegy written in a Country Churchyard*, 1751. David G. Taylor (see note 1) identifies the red-cloaked figure in *Edge of a Wood* as wearing a tricorn hat which went out of fashion by *c*.1780, and suggests the red cape is a riding cloak of *c*.1750.

13　Pike Watts wrote to Constable on 2 Oct 1815 that '…the Artist's view of Nature now presents the admired October tints, which adorn the ruralscenery' (R.B. Beckett ed., *John Constable's Correspondence: Patrons, Dealers and Fellow Artists*, Ipswich 1966, IV, p.44).

14　Constable was due to deliver the picture to his uncle after the close of the Academy exhibition (usually the end of June or early July), but his uncle died on 29 July. As *Edge of a Wood* has very plausibly been identified by Jennifer Thompson (see note 4) as the painting sold as Lot 51 in the sale of Constable's estate, Foster, 16 May 1838, either it was never delivered to Pike Watts owing to this failing health, or it was returned to Constable shortly after his death.

15　See note 6 for versions of *Helmingham Dell* based on a large drawing made by Constable in 1800 (Reynolds 1996, no.00.1).

16　I am grateful to Sarah Cove for confirming that *A Woodland Landscape* is painted on millboard (laid onto a cradled mahogany panel), see S. Cove, '*Woodland Landscape*, Condition & Treatment Report' 2012. The board has seven pinholes but these might relate to Constable pinning the study to a wall for consultation when working on *Edge of a Wood (A Wood; Autumn)* rather than holes made when pinning the work onto another, firmer surface to support it whilst painting in the open air. Furthermore, whilst millboard is a surface Constable had first adopted *c*.1809 specifically with *plein-air* work in mind, as Sarah Cove points out Constable was using this same support in 1819 – only three years after *Woodland Landscape* – for a compositional study in oils, the *Sketch for 'The Opening of Waterloo Bridge'* (V&A; Reynolds, 1984, no.19.23).

SAMUEL PALMER 1805–1881

Landscape – Twilight

Oil and tempera with pen and ink on panel
10½ × 15 inches · 265 × 380 mm
Painted in the early 1830s

COLLECTIONS
Probably, John Giles, a cousin of the artist,
1811–1880;
Probably, Giles sale, Christie's, 2 February
1881, lot 619, (bought by The Fine Art
Society);
Richard Budgett, acquired *c*.1890;
and thence by descent, 2014.

LITERATURE
Frederick George Stevens, *Notes on a collection of drawings, paintings and etchings by the
late Samuel Palmer*, 1881, pp.5 & 15;
Raymond Lister, *Catalogue raisonné of the
works of Samuel Palmer*, 1988, p.103, catalogue
no.216 (where incorrectly dated);
To be published by Colin Harrison in
his forthcoming book on Palmer for the
Ashmolean Museum as well as in his
projected revision of Raymond Lister's
catalogue raisonné.

EXHIBITED
Probably, London, Royal Academy, 1834,
no.419, *"Landscape – Twilight"*;
London, Fine Art Society, *A Collection
of Drawings, Paintings and Etchings
by the Late Samuel Palmer*, 1881, no.7 as
"Twilight";
Arts Council, *Samuel Palmer and his Circle:
The Shoreham Period*, 1956, no.42;
Arts Council, *Samuel Palmer and his Circle:
The Shoreham Period*, 1957, no.63;
Sheffield, Graves Art Gallery, *Samuel Palmer*,
1961, no.7;
Oxford, on loan to the Ashmolean Museum,
Oxford, 1984–1987.

Landscape – Twilight is a work of extraordinary power, beauty and importance
representing a culmination of the work
Samuel Palmer produced whilst living in the
Kent village of Shoreham. Shoreham was
physically and intellectually removed from
London, allowing Palmer to initially explore
a range of visionary subjects inspired by the
work of William Blake. By 1830 Palmer's
work had become less abstract and more
classical and naturalistic in its approach as
he attempted to find a commercial voice.
Landscape – Twilight was executed at this
crucial transitional moment. Whilst Palmer
constructs a pastoral landscape of shepherd
and his flock seated above a view of a
sweeping valley, the painting is executed
with a bold, artificial palette adding a visionary quality entirely typical of his earliest
Shoreham works. A lyrical evocation of
landscape and essay in the numinous qualities of nature executed at a crucial moment
of change in Palmer's work, this painting is
a masterpiece of European Romanticism.
Landscape – Twilight is in terms of condition,
provenance and history the most important of Palmer's oil landscapes left in
private hands.

Samuel Palmer moved to the village of
Shoreham in 1826 and lived there permanently until he bought a house in London in 1832.
Palmer later wrote of this period: 'forced
into the country by illness, I lived afterwards
for about seven years at Shoreham, in Kent,
with my father, who was inseparable from
his books… There, sometimes by ourselves,
sometimes visited by friends of congenial
taste, literature, and art and ancient music
wiled away the hours, and a small independ-
ence made me heedless, for the time, of
further gain; the beautiful was loved for
itself.'[1] Encouraged by other members of the
Ancients, a group of like-minded artists and
friends who met from 1824, Palmer produced
a series of severely primitive works inspired
by William Blake.

By 1830 Palmer's mystical view of nature
was being modified by the influence of John
Linnell, who urged him to work directly
from the landscape:

Samuel Palmer
Drawing for 'The Bright Cloud', *c.1831–2*
Indian ink and wash with scratching out
10 × 10¾ inches · 227 × 303 mm
© Tate, London 2014

Samuel Palmer
The Weald of Kent, 1833–4
Watercolour and gouache
7⅜ × 10⅝ inches; 187 × 270 mm
Yale Center for British Art, Paul Mellon Collection

Mr Linnell tells me that by making studies of the Shoreham scenery I could get a thousand a year directly. Tho' I am making studies for Mr Linnell, I will, God help me, never be a naturalist by profession.[2]

The results were, as the quotation implies, never as prosaic or commercial as Linnell might have hoped, and, in the more finished works, such as *Landscape – Twilight*, Palmer invests nature with a visionary significance instead of attempting to represent pure landscape. As William Vaughan notes in the essay on *Landscape – Twilight* that follows, Palmer: 'believed that the natural world was to be understood through the imagination, and that simple observation without this was an empty transcription of forms.' Palmer saw landscape painting as a way of conveying something of far greater significance both emotionally and spiritually than simply the construction of a picturesque view.

As David Bindman has pointed out Palmer's conception of rural England was similar to that of William Wordsworth, particularly as expressed in Wordsworth's *The Excursion* of 1814:

… the essence of the English landscape lay for Wordsworth in a mystical connection between nature, man and God, utterly opposed to the nation created by the 'new' Whigs, utilitarians and radicals… the linchpin of this mythical England was the 'Pastor', the country vicar who brought civility and godliness to the countryside, binding the immemorial past with the present. The bond between God and man is represented by the omnipresent church spire, making an organic connection between the village and 'the swelling hills and spacious plains' around it.[3]

For much of 1830 the countryside around Shoreham was in turmoil, with the 'Captain Swing' riots and wide spread rick-burning. Palmer feared that the pastoral landscape with which he identified so closely would be destroyed by political changes and reforms to the established church. As Colin Harrison has pointed out these shifts 'profoundly affected Palmer's art, as religious subjects gave way to the pastoral.'[4] *Landscape – Twilight* brings together all the elements which were central visual motifs of Palmer's work around 1830: the seated pastoral figure; a flock of sheep; boldly constructed flowering trees; the floor of a valley; a golden sunset and church spire. This is a landscape of continuity and nostalgia, a celebration of a way of life which Palmer felt was under threat. It is notable that Palmer places a spire at the heart of the composition – despite Shoreham church being one of the few in Kent without a spire – its presence acts as a reminder of the unity of nature, nation and religion exerted by the Anglican Church. It is therefore a composition which unites Palmer with the wider themes of Romantic landscape painting across Europe.

Twilight. Landscape is worked in both tempera and oil and areas, such as the lattice work of fields in the valley floor, with pen and ink. This was a technique Palmer learnt from William Blake and was directly related to early Italian painting. The medium allowed Palmer to achieve a luminosity of effect – the rich impasto handling of the glowing sky and deep blues of the distant hills – whilst retaining a quality of his drawings in gouache and watercolour. The trees on the right of the composition are built up with an abstraction and boldness which recalls *The Magic Apple Tree* in the Fitzwilliam Museum, Cambridge. Throughout the composition Palmer has worked areas with pen and ink adding a graphic quality which recalls the great monochrome ink drawings of *c*.1831–2. In no other painting of this period does Palmer combine the rich atmospheric effects of sunset, bold design of his great Shoreham watercolours and technical innovations of Blake.

Landscape – Twilight was probably painted for exhibition, whilst Palmer submitted several works with generic titles which could describe the present work to exhibitions in the early 1830s, it has not been conclusively linked to a specific known exhibited work. The first documented owner of the *Landscape – Twilight* is John Giles, Palmer's cousin, and it can be identified with some certainty as lot 619 in Giles's posthumous sale.[5] Giles was one of the 'Ancients' although he was not a painter, but a stockbroker by profession and helped look after Palmer's often precarious financial affairs, managing, on occasion, to act as a buffer between Palmer and his father-in-law, John Linnell. *Landscape – Twilight* was acquired by the Fine Art Society at the Giles sale and included in their pioneering 1881 exhibition devoted to Palmer's works.[6] It was then acquired at some stage before about 1890 by Richard Budgett and other than being loaned to the Ashmolean Museum in Oxford during the 1980s, it has remained virtually unseen until now with Budgett's descendants.

Samuel Palmer wrote to his friend, the painter George Richmond in October 1834: *I feel more energetic and ambitious for excellence in art than ever, but yet I hope with a more innocent and less selfish enthusiasm.*[7]

This statement came shortly before his marriage and trip to Italy, the last moment

Palmer was producing works inspired by his time at Shoreham. *Landscape – Twilight* stands as the greatest of these works: a pure distillation of Palmer's beatific vision of landscape. The combination of pastoral repose, stupendous visual effects and lyrical beauty make this work a monument of Romanticism; an assessment amplified by its untouched condition – *Landscape – Twilight* has seemingly not been cleaned in the last 100 years – and uninterrupted provenance from Palmer's cousin, John Giles.

We are very grateful to Colin Harrison and Professor William Vaughan for their help in cataloguing this work.

NOTES

1 Ed. Raymond Lister, *The Letters of Samuel Palmer*, Oxford, 1974, II, p.824.
2 Ed. Raymond Lister, *The Letters of Samuel Palmer*, Oxford, 1974, I, p.36.
3 David Bindman, 'The Politics of Vision: Palmer's *Address to the Electors of West Kent*, 1832', in ed. William Vaughan, *Samuel Palmer 1805–1881: Vision and Landscape*, exh.cat., London (British Museum), 2005, p.30.
4 Colin Harrison, 'Later Shoreham (1830–35)', in ed. William Vaughan, *Samuel Palmer 1805–1881: Vision and Landscape*, exh. cat., London (British Museum), 2005, p.137.
5 Christie's, 2 February 1881, lot 619.
6 *A Collection of Drawings, Paintings and Etchings by the Late Samuel Palmer*, 1881, no.7 as 'Twilight'.
7 Ed. Raymond Lister, *The Letters of Samuel Palmer*, Oxford, 1974, I, p.64.

above left: Samuel Palmer *A Hilly Scene, c.1826*
Watercolour, ink and tempera, varnished on panel
8¼ × 5⅜ inches · 209 × 136 mm
© Tate, London 2014

above: Detail from *Landscape – Twilight*

Samuel Palmer *Landscape – Twilight*
by William Vaughan

Samuel Palmer is best known for his original and vivid images of the English countryside, painted during that time that he was living, as a young man, in the Kent Village of Shoreham, between 1826 and 1835.

Landscape – Twilight is a fine example of Palmer's work from that time. While not a literal view of Shoreham, it is clearly inspired by the location. The village nestles in the valley of the river Darent, surrounded by wooded hills. This picture shows a view over such a valley, seen in the glimmering light of departing day. In the foreground a young girl rests, observing the scene. She is surrounded by a flock of sheep and appears to be a shepherdess. (Palmer has also added some oxen for good measure). Such a subject is highly typical for Palmer. There are many pictures he painted at the time expressing a similar ethos, such as *the Pastoral Scene* of 1835 now in the Ashmolean Museum Oxford (fig.1).

Palmer frequently described such works as pastorals. In doing this he was drawing on a venerable tradition reaching back to classical antiquity. He was a great admirer of the Roman Poet Virgil, who had set the tone for idyllic rural imagery in his *Eclogues*. Like other poets and painters before him, Palmer saw the pastoral as the means of evoking an ideal rural existence, a life of ease and tranquility to be set against the hectic materialism of the city and the modern age. Indeed, his decision to leave London for Shoreham in 1826 had been driven by a desire to discover some glimpses of a lost golden age in the countryside. For a time he thought he had found this. He once referred to Shoreham and its surrounds as his 'valley of vision'.

Palmer's idealized approach to rural life set him on a different path to contemporaries such as John Constable and his own

opposite:
Detail from *Landscape – Twilight*

right: [fig.1] Samuel Palmer
A Pastoral Scene, 1835
Oil on panel · 11¾ × 15¾ inches · 300 × 400 m
© Ashmolean Museum, University of Oxford

mentor, John Linnell who were exploring a naturalistic approach to landscape painting. "I will, God help me, never be a naturalist by profession" he wrote to his friend George Richmond in 1828.[1] Inspired by the visionary poet and painter William Blake, he believed that the natural world was to be understood through the imagination, and that simple observation without this was an empty transcription of forms. He aligned himself with Plato (a favourite author for him), who believed that the visible world was but a reflection of a higher reality beyond. It was the intimation of that higher reality that Palmer sought to evoke, using means that went beyond naturalistic representation.

One consequence of Palmer's interest was an emphasis on mood and sentiment in works. It encouraged him to look for particular effects of light that might suggest the mysterious and strange in nature. In *Landscape – Twilight* a meditative effect is achieved by the scene being shown as evening approaches. It is the end of the day, and humans and animals are going to their rest. He has dwelt in particular on the mysterious silhouette in the centre of the picture, that emerges as the sun goes down behind the brow of the hill.

Twilight was favourite time for Palmer. He painted the subject many times during his years at Shoreham. It was only rivalled in number by his moonlight scenes – which show a similar fascination with experiencing everyday scenery transformed by effects of low lighting. In is sign of his interest that six of the twenty two pictures he exhibited at the Royal Academy while living at Shoreham have the word 'twilight' in their title. It is quite possible that the present work is one of these. Works entitled 'Landscape.

Twilight' were shown in three successive exhibitions between 1832 and 1834.[2] Twilight was also sufficiently important to Palmer for him to celebrate it in verse. During his early years – particularly after his meeting with Blake in 1824, he devoted much time to writing poems on pastoral themes. One of these – which is drafted in his one surviving sketchbook from 1824 – is called 'Twilight Time'. While not altogether a success as a poem, it contains some poignant passages, and is an interesting indicator of the artist's ideas about that time of day. It begins with an evocation of evening:

And now the trembling light
Glimmers behind the little hills, and corn,
Lingring as loth to part …

He goes on to imagine looking down on a village at this time of day, much as in the picture under discussion here. The witness of the scene

shall look o'er yonder grassy hill,
At this village, safe and still.

Then, a few lines later, Palmer introduces the idea that such a scene has a visionary intensity quite unlike that of midday views.

Methinks the lingering, dying ray
Of twilight time, doth seem more fair,
And lights the soul up more than day
When wide-spread sultry sunshines are.[3]

This idea is close in sentiment to those expressed by Wordsworth in his *Intimations of Immortality* in which man's life is compared to the course of a day, and where the growing child gradually moves away from the vision of eternity, whence he came, to 'fade into the light of common day'. Palmer certainly knew Wordsworth's work well and sympathized with the Platonic vision expressed in this poem. However it is not dawn but twilight that draws his

attention. He sees the departing light as providing the vision of a world beyond. Addressing the 'glimm'ring light' of twilight directly he exclaims:

O thou that unto me dost seem more like
The dawning of a blissful day in heaven
Than the last close of one on this gross earth.[4]

Visually Palmer appears to have been set on this track by a work of William Blake's that he saw at the artist's house and later possessed. This is the set of wood engravings made by Blake to illustrate a pastoral poem by Ambrose Phillips in the edition of *The Pastorals of Virgil* produced by Robert Thornton in 1821. In making the wood engravings Blake adopted a method – unusual at the time – of showing the white lines cut into the block by the graver as positive values. The result was that the rustic imagery appeared to be illuminated by a low glimmering light (fig.2). It remains a matter of conjecture as to whether Blake deliberately intended to suggest this effect. But there is no doubt that Palmer responded to the prints as though they were twilight scenes. When studying them carefully in 1824 he wrote:

They are visions of little dells, and nooks and corners of Paradise; … There is in all such a mystic and dreamy glimmer as penetrates and kindles the inmost soul, and gives complete and unreserved delight, unlike the gaudy daylight of this world.[5] Certainly Palmer aimed to emulate this 'mystic and dreamy glimmer' in his own twilight scenes.

While Palmer's aim with his twilight and nocturnal scenes remained constant during his time in Shoreham, his methods of effecting them gradually changed. Gradually he moved from the dramatic primitivism of the time when he was first inspired by Blake, to a more conventional treatment. The change can be illustrated by contrasting a twilight scene made in 1825 (fig.3) – the year before he moved to Shoreham to a pastoral dateable to 1835 (fig.1).

The *Late Twilight* of 1825 shows a village nestling beneath a hill in the gloaming. The pastoral theme is introduced by the sleeping shepherd in the foreground. Heavily inspired by Blake's engravings and by the prints of Durer and his contemporaries in the sixteenth century, Palmer has designed the whole in a highly centralized manner with forms magnified and strong contrasts of black and white. The *Pastoral* of 1835, by contrast, has far gentler forms and softer shading. The design, too, is far more conventional, with clear foreground, middle ground and background as was conventional in landscapes of the period.

Unfortunately few of Palmer's works

COLINET.

[fig.2] William Blake
Illustration to Ambrose Philips's
'Imitation of Eclogue 1'
in Thornton's 'Pastorals of Virgil',
1821
Wood engraving
1¼ × 2⅞ inches · 32 × 73 mm
© The Trustees of the British Museum

from the Shoreham period are firmly date-able. But those few that are suggest that his most visionary and primitivistic work was done prior to 1830, and that there was an increasing move towards technical conventionality in the mid-1830s.

There are both material and psychological reasons for this change. When Palmer first went to Shoreham he had recently received a small legacy from his maternal grandfather. This enabled him to live for some years on his own means – albeit frugally. The fact that few of his works sold at this time was therefore not a crucial matter to him. He was able pursue his own way unhindered – presumably in the hope that in time he could win round critics and the public. By the early 1830s, however, funds were getting short. In 1834 he complained of experiencing a 'most unpoetical and unpastoral kind of poverty'.[6] He had to focus more on earning a living. He took up teaching, and also aimed more seriously at success through exhibition. It is noticeable that his move towards greater conventionality seems to have paid off in terms of getting works accepted for exhibition. Between 1826 and 1831 he only had works accepted by the Academy on two occasions. From 1832 onwards he was accepted by the Academy every year. By the time he left Shoreham eighteen works had been shown. However, even though his pictures became more prevalent in the Academy, they still did not sell. After 1835 he abandoned Shoreham subjects altogether and started exhibiting scenes of areas better known for their natural beauty, such as Devon and North Wales.

The psychological reasons for the change relate more to Palmer's attitude to rural life. In the early years at Shoreham he appears to have seen the village as a paradise on earth.

[fig.3] Samuel Palmer *Late Twilight, 1825*
Pen & dark brown ink with brush in sepia mixed
with gum arabic, varnished · 7⅛ × 9⅜ inches · 180 × 238 mm
© Ashmolean Museum, University of Oxford

[fig.4] After Gaspard Dughet
Landscape in the Roman Campagna, after 1670
Oil on canvas · 28¾ × 38¾ inches · 730 × 984 mm
© Dulwich Picture Gallery, 2014

However life in the countryside was far from tranquil at that time and unrest was growing as labourers became increasingly ground down by economic troubles and the effects of the modernization of farming methods. The uprisings of 1830s – notably the notorious 'captain swing' riots where farm machinery was smashed and hay ricks burned – affect the Shoreham area of Kent along with other places. If this showed that Shoreham was hardly a paradise on earth, there were further problems ahead when the Reform Bill of 1832 removed much of the political power of the rural communities. Palmer was a passionate opponent of the Reform Bill – writing a hysterical pamphlet against it. Such events did nothing to dim Palmer's love for the countryside and nature. But it brought home to him the fact that the old way of life that he treasured in the countryside was under threat and largely gone for ever. This encouraged a growing sense of nostalgia in the treatment of rural scenes. The ecstatic vision of his early Shoreham years gave way to a more regretful and meditative mood.

Landscape. Twilight would seem to fit into the post-1830 period. Like the Pastoral in the Ashmolean it is more conventional in composition. Indeed, they share a very similar design, with framing trees looking out to a middle ground hill or rock, and then to a distance behind. It is a sign of this return to conventionality that the model for this kind of landscape composition appears to be one of the masters of classical seventeenth century. This is the French painter Gaspar Dughet, whose work Palmer had studied in Dulwich. (fig.4) Like Claude and Poussin, Dughet lived in Rome and specialized in classicizing views of the Roman Campagna.

This particular work in Dulwich seems to have formed a specific point of departure. Although this format is a standard one, its particular treatment has special affinities with Dughet, especially the dominating effect of the hill rising above the horizon line in the central ground. It may have been that Palmer was returning here to a more conventional compositional type in the hope of making his work more saleable. On the other hand, the picture is quite different from the Dughet in its lighting effects and mood. Here Palmer is still very much himself.

Though the motif of the rock relates to Dughet, it seems to connect this picture also with a series of designs that Palmer made that show a similar rock with the sea beyond. The Pastoral at the Ashmolean is one of these, and there are others in the Tate, at Yale and in the British Museum.[7] These have tended to be dated 1834–5 for a particular reason. This is that they all show the sea. Palmer made his first trip to Devon in 1834, and it is supposed that these pictures show the effect of this visit. It is even supposed that the rock relates to Combe Martin bay that Palmer had admired in an engraving prior to going to Devon. The closeness of the rock motif in the present work to that in the Oxford *Pastoral* and the other might lead one to suppose that this work, too, is from that period. If this is the case it might well be the the 'Landscape. Twilight' that Palmer exhibited at the Royal Academy in 1835. However, it should be recalled that there is no sea in this work, and it might be that it is the connection with Dughet that is more important. Whichever is the case, all the evidence in the work points to a date after 1830.

The picture is painted using a combination of oil and tempera, a process Palmer habitually used in the mid-thirties. Prior to 1830 Palmer had affected a scorn of oil painting – inspired to some degree by Blake who associated it with the materialism of post-medieval art. This mixed media approach was later abandoned by Palmer, first for conventional oil painting and later for watercolour, which became the prevailing painting medium of his later years.

The picture came from Palmer's family, which points to it not having been sold, despite having been clearly intended for exhibition. This again is typical of works from the mid-1830s.

Landscape – Twilight is a beautiful, poignant, scene, painted at a time when Palmer was giving Shoreham one last chance, and hoping still to convey something of his unique vision of twilight to the public.

NOTES

1　Ed. Raymond Lister, *The Letters of Samuel Palmer*, Oxford, 1974, II, p.36.
2　A. H. Palmer, *The Life and Letters of Samuel Palmer, Painter and Etcher*, London 1892, p.406.
3　The verses occur in the sketchbook with many alterations. I have used the form transcribed in Mark Abley, *The Parting Light: Selected Writings of Samuel Palmer*, Manchester, 1985, p.133.
4　Abley, p.136.
5　A.H. Palmer, *Life and Letters*, pp.15–16.
6　*Letters of Samuel Palmer*, p.62.
7　Raymond Lister, *Catalogue Raisonné of the Works of Samuel Palmer*, Cambridge, 1988 cat.214, p.102.

DANIEL MACLISE RA 1806–1870
The Prince de Talleyrand

Pencil · 7 × 4¾ inches · 180 × 115 mm
Signed 'Alfred Croquis' (lower left), also
inscribed 'Talleyrand' (lower right)
Drawn c.1832

ENGRAVED
Lithographed by Engelmann, Graf, Coindet,
& Co. for *Fraser's Magazine for Town and
Country*, "Gallery of Literary Characters
no.XXXII," vol.VII, no.XXXVII, January 1833.

This is the original drawing by the Irish
artist Daniel Maclise – using the pseudonym
Alfred Croquis – for the engraved image
included in the series of notable characters
he created for *Fraser's Magazine* in the 1830s.
Fraser's Magazine, founded in 1830 by William
Maginn, used satire and ridicule to forward a
campaign for progressive social and economic reform. It also offered a platform for
advanced literary and intellectual comment,
publishing the early work of such authors as
Thackeray and Carlyle. Maclise's caricatures
were highly novel and executed with great
wit and elegance. His predominantly linear
style was well adapted to the medium of the
print and the majority were executed with a
lithographic pen.[1]

Charles Maurice de Talleyrand-Périgord
was successfully foreign minister under
Napoleon and Louis XVIII, who continually
pursued a peaceful settlement to conflict
in Europe and was a leading figure at the
Congress of Vienna in 1815. Talleyrand was
the French ambassador to London from
1830 to 1834 and played a major role in
the London Conference which effectively
achieved the recognition of Belgium as
an independent state. Maclise's highly
evocative pencil drawing was made during
Talleyrand's stay in London.

The present drawing was published

as a lithograph in the magazine with an
accompanying character sketch written
by Magnin. As William Bates noted in his
publication of *The Maclise Portrait-Gallery
of Illustrious Literary Characters*:
*The portrait by Maclise before us is certainly
sufficiently hideous, reminding one of a morbid
preparation in spirits, or one of those objects
of natural history which we see in glass cases,
impaled on a pin. Still, it is an admirable
drawing, and probably hardly caricatured as to
likeness … A most characteristic sketch, of the
wonderful old man?*[2]

Dante Gabriel Rossetti noted in the
Academy that:
*One picture stands out from the rest in mental
power, and ranks Maclise as a great master of
tragic satire. It is that which grimly shows us
the senile torpor of Talleyrand, as he sits in
after-dinner sleep between the spread board and
the fire-place, surveyed from the mantel-shelf by
the busts of all the sovereigns he had served.*[3]

Rossetti concluded his careful description of the print by observing:
*The is picture is more than a satire; it might
be called a diagram of Damnation; a ghastly
historical verdict which becomes the image of
man for ever.*

Fully signed by Maclise using his
pseudonym Alfred Croquis, this drawing
is an important survival demonstrating
Maclise's skill as a draughtsman and acuity
as a satirist.

NOTES
1 Richard Ormond, *Daniel Maclise 1806 – 1870*,
exh.cat. London (National Portrait Gallery),
1972, p.46.
2 William Bates, *The Maclise Portrait-Gallery
of "Illustrious Literary Characters" with Memoirs*,
London, 1883, p.154.
3 *The Academy*, April 15, 1871.

Baron François Gérard
Charles Maurize de Talleryand, Prince de Bénévent, 1808
Oil on canvas · 83⅞ × 57⅞ inches · 2130 × 1470 mm
Metropolitan Museum of Art, New York
Purchase, Mrs Charles Wrightsman, Gift 2012
© 2014 The Metropolitan Museum of Art
/ Art Resource / Scala, Florence

Engelmann, Graf, Coindet, & Co. after A. Croquis
Talleyrand, author of 'Palmerston, une comedie de deux ans'
Lithograph, 1833

Alfred Croquis

Talleyrand

RICHARD JAMES LANE 1800–1872

Queen Victoria

Pencil and watercolour
7½ × 6 inches · 190 × 153 mm
Drawn 1837

ENGRAVED
Lithograph by Richard Lane, published June 21, 1837, by J. Dickinson and J. Graf, printer to the Queen, 'Her Most Excellent Majesty the Queen'. Published to celebrate Victoria's accession to the throne the previous day.

Richard Lane was the most fashionable and successful portrait lithographer of the early nineteenth century and he executed a number of printed portraits of Queen Victoria. This exquisitely rendered profile drawing was made in preparation for a print of the young Queen Victoria which was published the day after her accession on 20th June 1837. A rare survival (the only other recorded slightly later example is in the Royal Collection[1]) and of outstanding quality, this delicate portrait shows the young queen at the beginning of her long reign and formed the basis of a hugely popular lithograph.

At the age of sixteen Lane was apprenticed to the line engraver Charles Heath. After completing his apprenticeship he worked as an engraver for some years, and in 1827 produced a print after Sir Thomas Lawrence's Red Riding Hood. By this time he had become dissatisfied with the commercialization of engraving and had abandoned it for lithography, a process Heath had been one of the first to practise in Britain. He first exhibited at the Royal Academy in 1824 and continued exhibiting there regularly until his death, and also occasionally at the Suffolk Street Gallery. He was elected an ARA in 1827. Not long before this he had dedicated his Studies of Figures by Gainsborough (1825) to the president of the Royal Academy, Sir Thomas

Lawrence. Lane produced most of the plates of this work in tinted lithography in imitation of Gainsborough's crayon originals, many of which were drawn on tinted paper and heightened with white. The outcome was one of the most remarkable applications of tinted lithography in the 1820s.

Lane's specialism was portraiture, and he produced hundreds of lithographs of this kind, including portraits of members of the royal family, leading artists and actors, and other notable figures, among them Lord Byron. The quality of his portrait lithography was reflected in the fees he charged, which in 1849 were sometimes as high as £100.

Victoria first sat for him in 1829 when she was a ten-year-old princess – the drawing is now in the Royal Collection – he then made drawings of her shortly after she became queen in 1837, when he was appointed Lithographer to the Queen, and three years later to the Prince Consort. In each of the prints the queen is seen in profile, her hair dressed in a distinctive style – some show her wearing a Ferronière, a pendant on her forehead, as in the present drawing and others a wreath of flowers – with a plaited bun. Given the high quality of the present drawing, it may well be identifiable with one exhibited at the Royal Academy in 1838, possibly as no.590 'Profile of Her Majesty' and this is given further credence by the survival of a fragment of an old label dating this drawing to 1838.

Depictions of the young Queen Victoria are rare and this beautifully rendered, tinted profile drawing is an important addition to her iconography, made by the most important and celebrated lithographer of the day.

NOTES
1   Richard Ormond, *Early Victorian Portraits*, London, 1973, I, p.479, listed under '1829'.

R. J. Lane
Her Most Excellent Majesty the Queen
Lithograph on chine collé
Published June 21, 1837
10⅝ × 8¼ inches · 271 × 210 mm
© The Trustees of the British Museum

F. C. Lewis, after R. J. Lane
Her most Gracious Majesty the Queen
Hand-coloured stipple engraving
Published June 22, 1837
12 × 9⅞ inches · 306 × 250 mm
© The Trustees of the British Museum

DANIEL MACLISE RA 1806–1870

The Debut in London of Nicolò Paganini

Pencil
5½ × 4 inches · 140 × 102 mm
Drawn 1831

COLLECTIONS
Ambrose Poynter (1796–1886);
Charles Francis Bell, grandson of the above;
Edward Croft-Murray (1907–80),
acquired in 1938;
And by descent, to 1996;
Private collection, 2014.

LITERATURE
Richard Ormond, *Daniel Maclise 1806–1870*,
exh.cat., London and Ireland (National
Portrait Gallery and National Gallery of
Ireland), 1972, pp.40–41.

EXHIBITED
London, National Portrait Gallery and
Dublin, National Gallery of Ireland, *Daniel
Maclise*, 1972, no.36.

This engaging pencil study was made from life by the Irish artist Daniel Maclise at the debut of the Italian virtuoso violinist Nicolò Paganini in London on 3 June at the King's Theatre in London. Articles in *The Times* (including concert review, 4th June 1831) and *Playgoer* were among many which noted the astonishment shown by musicians on the stage and audience alike. Our study showing Paganini concentrating on his own playing – with a vignette of Paganini's left hand carefully posed in a complicated piece of fingering – whilst three members of the orchestra watching captivated. Apart from Paganini himself, Maclise captured the pianist, cellist and double-bass player who made up the continuo of the larger orchestra; they have been tentatively identified as: the cellist Robert Lindley, double bass player Domenico Dragonetti and another figure, possibly the violinist Nicolas Mori or possibly the conductor Sir George Smart.

Maclise seems to have used this sketch as a study for a larger highly finished drawing now in the V&A which in turn served as the basis for Richard Lane's lithograph entitled 'The Modern Orpheus' which communicated the frenetic – almost demotic – playing of Paganini which captivated audiences throughout Europe. Paganini behaved as a self-acknowledged genius, and was often credited as a musician with diabolical powers. Paganini wrote at the time of his English visit: 'Scores of portraits of me made by different artists have appeared in all the print shops.'[1]

This fascinating drawing – a document of one of the most remarkable musical evenings in London's musical life – belonged successively to the Ambrose Poynter the nineteenth-century architect, his grandson Charles Francis Bell, Keeper of Art at the Ashmolean Museum, Oxford and Edward Croft-Murray, the Keeper of Prints and Drawings at the British Museum.

Daniel Maclise
Debut in London of Nicolò Paganini, 1831
Pencil and wash, with touches of white chalk
14⅛ × 10¾ inches · 359 × 273 mm
© Victoria & Albert Museum, London, Forster Bequest

NOTES
1 Richard Ormond, *Daniel Maclise 1806–1870*,
exh.cat., London and Ireland (National
Portrait Gallery and National Gallery of
Ireland), 1972, p.40.

SIR EDWIN LANDSEER RA 1802–1873

Nicolò Paganini (1782–1840)

Pen and ink wash
9 × 7¾ inches · 230 × 188 mm
Dated on a backing sheet: April 16 1834
Drawn c.1831–34

Edwin Landseer, a hugely talented and instinctive draughtsman was greatly in demand amongst his social circle for his extempore drawings and caricatures and his studies of Nicolò Paganini were especially sought after. Paganini's debut in London in 1831 generated immense excitement and a number of artists depicted him in action; this catalogue includes a study by Daniel Maclise made at the performance which was turned into a popular lithograph. Paganini returned to London throughout his performing career and the present drawing seems to have been made by Landseer whilst Paganini was in London in 1834. Landseer has captured the drama inherent in Paganini's often frenzied performances, something which contemporaries were acutely aware of; the carefully articulated fingers of the left hand and the raised bow, ready to play, the intense gaze and bent knee also suggest the intensity of Paganini's performance.

Our drawing is one of a number of portraits of Paganini executed by Landseer. The first was made at a soirée given by Marguerite, Countess of Blessington, at Gore House in 1831. She and her lover Count d'Orsay were close friends of Landseer. The Blessington drawing, now in a private collection, depicts Paganini intensely playing the violin, as Richard Ormond has noted, Landseer has drawn Paganini: 'with an air of wrapt concentration, eyes staring, nose prominent, long hair streaming out over his shoulders. This is the picture of a man of genius transported by his art.'[1] Landseer produced other drawings of Paganini more or less based upon the same format and pose: a full-length study is in the collection of the Royal Academy of Music and a study close to the present drawing is preserved

in the City of Manchester Art Galleries.[2] The Blessington drawing was subsequently reproduced as a private lithographic plate by Charles Hulmandel in 1842; this suggests the popularity and longevity of Landseer's depiction of Paganini.

The present drawing is inscribed on its contemporary backing sheet 'April 16 1834', the date of a concert Paganini gave at the Adelphi Theatre in London. The programme of public concerts over three nights included a number of works composed and performed by Paganini, including his famous 'Sonata Militare: performed entirely on one string, (the fourth).' Although Richard Ormond has dated all Landseer's drawings of Paganini to 1831, it seems just as likely that they date from slightly later and the present study could well have been completed in 1834. Landseer was a master of caricature and the present dynamic drawing depicts Paganini as he was seen by a contemporary audience: the embodiment of Romantic genius.

NOTES

1 Richard Ormond, *Edwin Landseer: The Private Drawings*, Norwich, 2009, p.161.
2 Richard Ormond, *Edwin Landseer: The Private Drawings*, Norwich, 2009, pp.156–165.

GEORGE RICHMOND RA 1809–1896

Frédéric Chopin (1810–1849)

Pencil · 13¼ × 10⅝ inches · 335 × 270 mm
Cropped inscription 'Richmond'
Drawn *c.*1848

Writing in her diary whilst in Paris, the amateur singer Fanny Erskine, recorded several meetings with the composer Frédéric Chopin in January 1848. One evening she visited the house of her distant relation, Katherine Erskine, where she met Chopin, his Norwegian pupil Thomas Tellefsen and the British painter George Richmond:
A little select party there. Richmond – Chopin – Miss Trotter, Tellephson & ourselves – Richmond was so pleasant & talking of the benefits to the character of trail & having to wait & expect what we earnestly desire to obtain & of the way in which it is doubly prized after... Chopin played for a long long time so splendidly & was quite frisky after, making rabbits on the wall & shewing off his various accomplishments.[1]

Eugène Delacroix
Frédéric Chopin, c.1838
Oil on canvas · 18⅛ × 15 inches · 460 × 380 mm
Musée du Louvre, Paris © 2014
Photo: Scala, Florence

George Richmond was in Paris over the Christmas of 1847 for a short two week visit and it seems likely that whilst there he completed this incisive portrait of Chopin, then terminally ill. Characteristic of Richmond's rapid and intelligent portraiture, this sensitive study is an unpublished and previously unrecorded depiction of the great Romantic composer.

The beginning of 1848 was a bleak moment for Chopin; he had recently ended his decade-long relationship with George Sand and was on the eve of delivering his final public performance in Paris. Fanny Erskine, who was travelling with her aunt Mrs Mary Rich and are recorded staying at the house of Chopin's British patrons, the Schwabes, in the Champs-Elysées, gives a vivid description of Chopin during their meetings at Katherine Erskine's house:
'he is such an interesting looking man but Oh! So suffering, & so much younger than I had expected. He exerted himself talking at dinner & seemed so interested in Mendelssohn & the honors paid to his memory in London but said there was something almost enviable in his fate dying in the midst of his family surrounded by love – & with his wife beside him – & having lived so purely happy a life – & he looked so sad. I felt for him for they say he is so lonely & obliged to even to go out for his Breakfast & suffering dreadfully from asthma...he grew quite playful & seemed to forget his suffering.'[2]

Richmond was staying with Katherine Erskine in Paris, the widow of James Erskine of Linlathen. In 1848 Richmond drew and engraved a portrait of Katherine Erskine's brother-in-law, the theologian, Thomas Erskine. He would go on to paint

Fanny Erskine, later Mrs Thomas Farrer.[3] Richmond left his own account of his meeting with Chopin in Paris in 1848 which was recounted by A.M.W. Stirling in 1926:
The great master was carried in from his bedroom, wrapped up in blankets sweating in the last stage of consumption; but directly he touched the piano, inspiration came back to him and the fire of life returned. He played and played, like a drifting dream, dainty themes like weft of gossamer, strains like the echo of a fairy's dance, and all the while his hacking cough cleft the grace of his fantasy with cruel reminder of the advance of death.[4]

Richmond's rapid, incisive study captures both Chopin's weak state of health, particularly in his gaunt, thin face and his latent energy, in his animated, penetrating eyes. Made the year before Chopin died, this portrait is an important addition to Chopin's iconography. The youthful figure of Delacroix's great 1828 double portrait of Chopin and George Sand had been replaced by a more world weary figure. As such this portrait is not only an important addition to Richmond's *oeuvre*, but a significant discovery for Chopin scholars.

NOTES

1   Ed. John Rink and Jim Samson, *Chopin Studies 2*, Cambridge, 1992, p.248.

2   Ed. John Rink and Jim Samson, *Chopin Studies 2*, Cambridge, 1992, p.247.

3   Raymond Lister, *George Richmond*, London, 1981, p.158.

4   A.M.W. Stirling, *The Richmond Papers*, London, 1926, p.7.

WILLIAM TURNER OF OXFORD 1782–1862

The Sands at Barmouth, North Wales

Watercolour
10⅛ × 14¼ inches · 257 × 362 mm
Signed 'W Turner Oxford' (lower right, over-mounted partially)
Painted 1832

COLLECTIONS
Private collection, 1972;
Jean Horsman, by 1987 to 1997;
Spink-Leger, London;
Private collection, USA, acquired from the above 1997, to 2014.

EXHIBITED
London, Society of Painters in Water-Colours, 1832, no.157, 6 guineas.

Writing in 1831, an anonymous reviewer of the annual exhibition at the Society of Painters in Water-Colours praised the work of William Turner of Oxford, noting that they were not well known or suited to the exhibition where the 'florid manner of colouring' of many works was 'so injurious to that sober style of landscape which is the object of Mr Turner's study, and in which he particularly excels.'[1] The reviewer went on to note:

His works are not only unobtrusive, but even uninviting, appearing at first sight rather sombre than gay, and to be known must be sought; but when sought, they are discovered to be worth the effort which engaged their acquaintance, being intelligent and replete with the sterling properties of landscape art.

The quiet, powerful landscapes of William Turner remain comparatively little known. This powerful sheet perfectly demonstrates the 'unobtrusive' and 'sombre' aspect of his work, but also underlines his exceptionally technical ability and the 'intelligence' of his vision.

William Turner first exhibited at the Royal Academy in 1807 and in January 1808 he became the youngest associate of the Society of Painters in Water Colours and in November a full member. His precocity was further recognized when he was chosen to preside at the inaugural meeting of the *Society for Epic and Pastoral Design*, a reincarnation of the *Sketching Society* which earlier included Thomas Girtin and John Sell Cotman as well as Varley among its members. This was the moment when Varley, 'at Millar, the Booksellers evening Converzatione', at which leading artists were gathered:

spoke violently of the merit of a young man who had been his pupil in learning to draw in watercolour and Reinagle said 'He had never before seen drawings equal to them'. His name Turner[2]

In 1810 one critic voiced the opinion, 'it is not flattery to say that he has outstripped his master.'[3] This must be on the basis of major works which are the climax of these early years such as the bleak and stormy *Scene near Woodstock*, exhibited in 1809 (Private collection, USA, formerly with Lowell Libson Ltd) and *Whichwood Forest, Oxfordshire* (Victoria and Albert Museum, London), which shows a dense yet animated forest interior in which a confined encounter with nature in an apparent state of tumult is contrasted with a distant glimpse of tranquillity. The technical and imaginative resources of this work are the fruit of Turner's study of both old and modern masters.

In about 1812 (the date when the Watercolour Society collapsed, then reformed in less exclusive guise, admitting oil paintings) Turner returned to

Oxfordshire, probably living initially at Shipton, and depending for his income on giving lessons, both in the University of Oxford and around the county. Teaching was to provide the basis of his income for the rest of his life. His subject matter expanded beyond his home territory with his regular summer sketching tours. He made a point of familiarizing himself with all the prime sites of the picturesque and made visits to the Lake District in 1814, Wales in 1817, and the Peak District in 1818. These followed a brief trip to Clifton Gorge and the Wye in 1808 or 1809.

In about 1824 Turner's cousin acquired a farm in the New Forest and Turner was a regular visitor. He exhibited scenes of that ancient woodland from 1827 and also began to explore the South Downs, which he depicted in sparse panoramic vistas overlooking Portsmouth harbour or Bowhill near Chichester. In keeping with the times, these could be monumental in scale. One of the occasional oils Turner continued to paint from time to time throughout his career, View of Portsmouth Harbour from Portsdown Hill, exhibited at the British Institution in 1841, measured 6 feet 7 inches wide, including the frame. This ambition culminated in Turner of Oxford's most spectacular exhibition watercolour *Near Lustleigh Cleeve, on the River Teign, Devonshire, Dartmoor in the distance*, which he showed at the Society of Painters in Water-Colours in 1832, (National Gallery of Art, Washington DC, formerly with Lowell Libson Ltd).

In the same year Turner showed this small, powerful view of Barmouth in North Wales. Like the considerably larger watercolour of Devon, the view of Barmouth with its brooding sky offered Turner the

opportunity to demonstrate his prodigious talents as a technician in watercolour. The small port of Barmouth, close to the mountains of Snowdonia, had long been included in the picturesque tours of North Wales. In John Britton's account of the town in his *The Beauties of England and Wales* of 1812, Barmouth, its adjacent landscape and river are thus described:

The river forms an arch of the sea, and when the estuary is full of water, the scenes which present themselves for some miles are truly picturesque. In the composition of the different views, scarcely any thing can be conceived wanting; every requisite for fine landscape; mountain and valley, rocks, meadows, woods, water, are here grouped, and arranged in the most beautiful order.[4]

In the present view Turner has deliberately eschewed the conventions of the picturesque; choosing the estuary when the river is almost empty and tide out to reveal an expanse of exposed sand, the thin blue line of the horizon and distant mountains and the large expanse of brooding sky. The reduced palette and depopulated landscape,

Turner has only included a few diminutive figures, add to the intensity and atmosphere of the view.

The critic John Ruskin came late to Turner's work, praising his landscapes in *Modern Painters* in 1851, for their: 'quiet and simple earnestness, and tender feeling.'[5] A perfect summation of Turner's achievement in his view of Barmouth which is celebration of the grandeur of landscape and climate and rejection of the artificiality of the picturesque. Although Turner of Oxford is far less famous than his contemporary namesake, J.M.W. Turner, both shared a prodigious ability as watercolourists and their technical invention enabled their compositions to transcend the purely topographical. In its subtlety, extraordinary technical virtuosity and profound beauty this picture is both amongst the greatest of Turner of Oxford's work, albeit of a small format, and an example of the imaginative and technical facility of British watercolourists in the first half of the nineteenth century.

NOTES

1 *Arnold's Library of the Fine Arts or Repertory of Painting, Sculpture, Architecture and Engraving*, London, 1831, 1, p.513.

2 ed. Kathryn Cave, *The Diary of Joseph Farington*, New Haven and London, 1982, 9, p.3209.

3 'Watercolour exhibitions', Ackermann's Repository of the Arts, Literature and Commerce, 3, July 1810, p.432.

4 John Britton, *The Beauties of England and Wales*, London, 1812, vol.XVII, part 1, p.951.

5 John Ruskin, *Modern Painters*, London, 1848, 1, p.69.

William Turner of Oxford
A View in Devon from Mannerton, 1832
Watercolour with scratching out and gum arabic
29½ × 42¾ inches · 750 × 1085 mm · In the original frame
National Gallery of Art, Washington DC
(formerly with Lowell Libson Ltd)

William Turner of Oxford *An April shower: A view from Binsey Ferry near Oxford looking towards Port Meadow and Godstow, 1842*
Watercolour over pencil heightened with gouache and scratching out
18 × 27 inches · 455 × 685 mm
Signed, also and signed and inscribed verso: 'No. 3 / W. Turner'
The Art Institute of Chicago (formerly with Lowell Libson Ltd)

JOSEPH MALLORD WILLIAM TURNER RA 1775–1851

A Distant View over Chambéry, from the North, with Storm Clouds

Watercolour
9¾ × 10¾ inches · 248 × 273 mm
Painted 1836

COLLECTIONS
John Edward Taylor;
Taylor sale, Christie's, 8th July 1912, lot 107
'A Mountainous Landscape: a town seen in
a valley, in the middle distance', (1100 gns to
Gibbs);
Horace Gibbs;
Mrs Willard Straight (née Dorothy Payne
Whitney, later Mrs Leonard K. Elmhirst),
acquired from or through Horace Gibbs in
1912, to 1942;
Mrs Robert B. Choate, Danvers MA, by 1946,
to 1983;
Leger Galleries, London;
Private collection, acquired from the above,
1984;
By descent, 2014.

LITERATURE
Walter Thornbury, *The Life and
Correspondence of J.M.W. Turner*, 1862, vol.1,
pp.229–231 (see also George Jones's anno-
tated copy of this book, formerly in the
possession of Frances Haskell, and now in
the Print Room at Tate Britain; this contains
Munro of Novar's own recollections of the
1836 tour);
A.J. Finberg, *The Life of J.M.W. Turner*, Oxford
1961, pp.361–2;
Selby Whittingham, News and Sales Record,
Turner Studies, Winter 1984, vol.4, no.2, p.62;
David Hill, *Joseph Mallord William Turner.
Le Mont-Blanc et la Vallée d'Aoste*, exh.cat.,
Museo Archeologico Regionale, Aosta, 2000,
pp.123, 271–2, no.14, (as 'Sallanches, 1836');
Andrew Wilton, *Turner in his time*, revised
edition, 2006, p.155.

EXHIBITED
New York, Metropolitan Museum,
1912–42 (on loan from Mrs Dorothy Whitney
Straight);
New York, Kende Galleries at Gimball Bros.,
1942, no.190;
Boston, Museum of Fine Arts, *Paintings,
Drawings and Prints by J. M. W. Turner, John
Constable and R. P. Bonington*, 1946, no.41 (lent
by Mrs Robert B. Choate);
London, Leger Galleries, *English
Watercolours*, 1984, no.2 (as 'An Alpine Valley,
probably the Val d'Aosta');
Toronto Art Gallery, *Turner and the Romantic
Landscape*, 1995;
Aosta, Museo Archeologico Regionale,
*Joseph Mallord William Turner: Le Mont-Blanc
et la Vallée d'Aosta*, July–October 2000, no.14
(as Sallanches).

This watercolour was painted during
Turner's tour of the Alps in 1836, an important journey that is now recognised as a
crucial watershed in the development of his
later style and working methods. The colour
studies he made during the tour are not
thought to be preliminary designs for future
commissions, but have been aptly described
by Professor David Hill as 'sufficient and
entire unto themselves'. In his account of
Turner's route, Professor Hill proposed
that the principal value of the sketches was
the use they 'served at the time, to focus
and structure the process of observation',
thereby intensifying the experience (Hill
2000, p.261).

Turner's objective in his 1836 travels was
to revisit an area he had first explored half
a lifetime ago. He was then sixty-one, but
as a twenty-seven year old he had rushed to
the Alps in 1802, during the short-lived Peace
of Amiens. Whereas, for most of Turner's
travels, we have little first-hand information
about his movements or his opinions of
the places he visited, the 1836 journey was
of quite a different character. For a start,
he was accompanied for much of it, which
was a circumstance he otherwise seems to
have preferred to avoid. His companion this
year was the young Scottish landowner,
Hugh Andrew Johnstone Munro of Novar
(1797–1864), whom he had known since
the later 1820s. By 1836 Munro was already
becoming the most dependable collector of
Turner's latest paintings. This was in itself
remarkable at a time when, increasingly, the
artist's pictures returned, unsold, at the end
of the annual Royal Academy exhibitions.
Munro's interests were wide-ranging, as
was his taste for art; his collection included
many works by his contemporaries, as well

as notable old master paintings (such as the *Madonna dei Candelabri* at the Walters Art Gallery in Baltimore, then attributed to Raphael). He was apparently also a talented amateur, though examples of his work are now rare.

In foregoing the pleasurable solitude usual on his travels, it is apparent that Turner was taking a paternal interest in his young patron, attempting to distract him from a potentially hazardous entanglement in politics (see Hill 2000, p.262). At the time Turner may also have felt somewhat beholden to Munro, who appears to have bank-rolled his stay in Venice in 1833. Presumably the wealthy Scotsman also largely subsidised their joint expenses in 1836.

Most usefully, Munro later provided short reports, with valuable details of the journey, both to John Ruskin in 1857, and to Walter Thornbury, the journalist who wrote one of the earliest biographies of Turner (1862). Combining these with Turner's own notebooks and his watercolour sketches, it is possible to reconstruct the outline of the tour, and get a sense of where the two men paused. Some of the material that Turner produced at various places, as described by Munro, can be identified precisely, whilst other items appear not to have survived. How some of this got separated from the bulk of Turner's personal studies, now in his bequest at Tate Britain, is a matter of speculation. The correspondence between Ruskin and Munro reveals that it came onto the market in the later 1850s via a foreign dealer, but unfortunately there is nothing more to record the precise source of the colour sketches.

Since it first appeared, the watercolour discussed here was readily associated with the 1836 tour to the Aosta valley because of the distinctive character of the colours Turner used, which can also be found in several of the other studies (see those discussed in Andrew Wilton, *The Life*

and Work of J.M.W. Turner, Fribourg 1979, pp.471–4, nos.1430–1456; the present watercolour was unknown to Wilton when he prepared that catalogue). Despite its evident connection with the Alpine tour, no specific subject was proposed until Professor Hill, in his 2000 exhibition catalogue, linked the scene with Sallanches, in the Arve Valley, to the north-west of Mont Blanc.

According to Munro, he and Turner had stopped at St Martin and Sallanches quite early in their route through the Alps, and it may have been a significant moment, though the accounts are somewhat muddled and conflicting. In a letter to Ruskin dated 14 November 1857, Munro said that he had not noticed Turner taking his colours out until they were actually in Switzerland, though he had himself worked in watercolour at Sallanches. Subsequently, however, in Thornbury's rather garbled version, Turner is described as having witnessed Munro struggling with a colour sketch at Sallanches. Rather than commenting on it, Turner tactfully 'took up a new drawing-pad that was lying near … and off he went to "see what he could do with it." He returned in about two hours with the paper squared into four sketches, each in a different stage of completion.' According to Thornbury, 'This was evidently his rough, kind way of showing an amateur friend the way of pushing forward a sketch.'

There are several sketches of Sallanches in the Turner Bequest (see TB CCCXLII 75, 76, 77; two of these are reproduced left; the third is Hill 2000, p.122, no.13). In these the lively outlines of the town and the distant mountains are worked in plumbago, the graphite medium described by Munro as Turner's preferred choice on the early stages of the journey. In his catalogue, Hill linked these three sketches with this watercolour and the anecdote just related (even though the paper on which the watercolour is painted is different from that used for the

J. M. W. Turner
Sallenche, 1836
Chalk and graphite · 9⅜ × 12⅛ inches · 237 × 310 mm
© Tate, London 2014, TB CCCXLII 75/D34277

J. M. W. Turner
Sallenche, 1836
Chalk and graphite · 9½ × 12 inches · 240 × 305 mm
© Tate, London 2014, TB CCCXLII 76/D34278

sketches). One of the telling details he identified for making a connection between these works was that the upper parts of one of the sketches bears traces of watercolour, indicating that this sheet had been placed below another where work on the sky had occasionally gone beyond the top edge of the uppermost work. The assumption was that the cloudy sky in the 'Sallanches' watercolour must have been the cause of these extraneous marks.

In setting out the topography in the image, Hill identified the view as from the Fours la Sallanches valley, looking over the church of St Jacques directly to the Aiguille de Varan. He notes that Turner had compressed the full sweep of the panorama of dramatic topography in his pencil sketches, and must therefore have similarly adjusted the range of mountains when painting the watercolour. However, there are noticeable differences between the shape of the peaks recorded in either media that suggest they may not actually depict the same place.

Nevertheless, Hill's analysis of Turner's technique is acute and passionate: 'It is a tour de force of energetic handling of paint, for the most part working broad passages of colour one up against another, and mixing and modulating directly on the paper, but always, and most impressively in the effects of cloud on the mountains, with an extraordinary control of the flow and drying of the paint' (Hill 2000, p.272).

As there are grounds for questioning the identification of the view as Sallanches, it is worth briefly considering its place in the sequence of watercolours produced during the tour. Munro of Novar noted that 'they were generally done in squarish sizes, perhaps as big as a large sheet of writing paper', but that some were 'cut up in smaller dimensions'. In fact Turner's 1836 watercolours were generally of a standard landscape format until he climbed above Chamonix towards Mont Blanc, whereupon the sheets he selected were squarish, measuring roughly 25 x 28 cms (see Hill 2000, nos.21, 23, 24, 25). If the view really is Sallanches, it would be the first of the sequence, but it feels quite different in mood from the Mont Blanc series.

Another group painted on sheets of the same size was made on the other side of Mont Blanc at Pre-Saint-Didier, in the Aosta valley (Hill 2000, nos.36–39). These last four works, with their sequential variations on the same viewpoint, might in fact better relate to the anecdote in which Turner set down instructive variations on a theme from which Munro might study his working process. Perhaps Thornbury misquoted or jumbled up Munro's narrative on this point?

As they pressed on down the Aosta valley the square format, or a slightly elongated version of its dimensions, became the norm both for Turner's more expansive pencil sketches and his colour studies, the larger sheets supplementing the rudimentary notes in his sketchbooks. The Fitzwilliam Museum in Cambridge owns a colour study that shares some of the same elements as the present watercolour (Hill 2000, no.54). Both are founded on the yellow-green base washes that darken into earthy ochre tones. The shadowy masses of the mountains are in each case given weight by a fairly concentrated blue, which is thinned and darkened in the sky to recreate the passage of rain clouds. In another work, a view of Aosta, formerly owned by J.E. Taylor (who may also have possessed this watercolour), the pattern through which the image was built up was roughly the same, but Turner also added prominent figures on the road, and scratched away at the painted surface to

Joseph Mallord William Turner
From Sarre looking towards Aymavilles,
Val d'Aosta, 1836
Watercolour and gouache
9⅜ × 11¾ inches · 237 × 298 mm
© Fitzwilliam Museum, Cambridge
Museum of Fine Arts, Boston

J. M. W. Turner
Mont Blanc and the Glacier des Bossons from
above Chamonix; Evening, 1836
Graphite and watercolour
10 × 11 inches · 256 × 280 mm
© Tate, London 2014, TB CCCLXIV 152/D35996

J. M. W. Turner
Mont-Blanc and Le Chetif looking over Pre-Saint
Didier in the Val d'Aosta, 1836
Watercolour
10 × 11 inches · 255 × 279 mm
© Tate, London 2014, TB CCCLXIV 121/D35964

introduce lively highlights (Museum of Fine Arts, Boston; see Hill 2000, no.59).

Another relevant watercolour, and one that bears perhaps the closest comparison is a view of Chambéry (Private collection; Hill 2000, no.78). Painted late in the tour, and related to sketches in the 'Fort Bard' sketchbook, it surveys the attractive historic city from the south-east, with heavy dark clouds bearing down to the peaks. The cathedral and the adjacent chateau of the counts and dukes of Savoie are rendered merely as a generalized mass of towered buildings amidst indications of a sprawling urban settlement. This indistinctness is curious and obviously a deliberate decision, because Turner had diligently recorded the architecture in the 1836 sketchbook. Furthermore, had he wanted to corroborate any of the newly acquired visual information, back in London he could have consulted the sketches he made of Chambéry in January 1829, on his way back from Rome that year (see Ian Warrell, *Turner's Sketchbooks*, 2014, p.147).

Several aspects in the south-east view of Chambéry can also be found in the watercolour considered here. They possess exactly the same palette range: the diluted greybrown used for the landmarks of the city; the zesty lemon highlights on the hillsides; the darkening blues of higher slopes; and the washed-out inkiness of the clouds. Common to both is a patch of solid blue to mark a shaded spur on the left hand side, as well as the shared sense of deep space, artfully created through successive planes of colour.

Going back to the 'Fort Bard' sketchbook, it is apparent that the watercolour can be related to the various views Turner made of Chambéry from the north (TB CCXCIV 20 verso, 21, 22, 23). The last two of these, especially, seem to provide the basis for the watercolour view. Typically, Turner has favoured a distant prospect that gives a better sense of the wider setting, seen from the outskirts, rather than a composition dealing only in the picturesque particularities of celebrated monuments, as favoured by some of his contemporaries. Indeed, earlier in the tour Munro recalled that Turner had anxiously sought to outshine the types of view made in Dijon by James Duffield Harding (1797/8–1863). Something of the same casual approach to Chambéry's historic core can also be found in the related colour study, and in both Turner neglected to work up the landmarks of the city centre. In this instance, the misty area, left blank at the heart of the image, may have left Turner with the option of giving the buildings fuller treatment at a later stage.

John Edward Taylor, the pre-eminent collector of Turner watercolours in the years following the artist's death, was the son of the founder of *The Manchester Guardian*. He began buying from Agnew's in the 1860s, with *The Blue Rigi* (Tate) among his earlier purchases. His other Turners included *The Red Rigi* (National Gallery of Victoria) acquired from John Ruskin. In 1892 Taylor gave 154 watercolours to The Whitworth Institute (now Whitworth Art Gallery), Manchester. These included 25 works by Turner, nearly all of them early works to go with the earlier British watercolours in the Whitworth; the only later work was *Fire at Fennings Wharf, on the Thames at Bermondsey* of c.1835. Two years later, in 1894, he gave a further selection of drawings to the Victoria and Albert Museum, London, including two late Swiss watercolours by Turner. Despite these gifts, however, it took twelve days for Christie's to disperse the remainder of Taylor's collection in July 1912. Of the 107 works by Turner Agnew's bought the first, *Longships Lighthouse*, 'and then the next 34 lots in succession before allowing Palser to have lot 77' (E. Joll, catalogue of the Turner exhibition held at Agnew's, 1967); despite this rare concession Agnew's went on to buy roughly two thirds of all the Turners in the sale, including both *The Blue Rigi* and *The Red Rigi*. *The Blue Rigi* sold for the enormous price of 2,700 guineas (it was to be acquired after a public appeal by the Tate in 2007 for £5.8m), while *The Red Rigi* fetched 2,100 guineas. The price of 1,100 guineas achieved by the present work was one of the highest achieved in the sale of Taylor's distinguished group of Turner watercolours. Mrs Willard Straight (née Dorothy Payne Whitney) acquired the present work, *Chambéry*, from or through H. Gibbs who purchased it at the Taylor sale in 1912. She also owned the watercolour of the *Val d'Aosta looking over Sallanches* (Museum of Fine Art, Boston) from the Taylor sale (lot 63) which had been one of Agnew's many purchases. Watercolours dateable to this tour are catalogued by Andrew Wilton in *The Life and Work of J. M. W. Turner*, 1979, nos. 1430–1456, and share a distinctive colouring 'applied in a rich, almost unctuous way' on sheets of paper which are typically almost square in format. Other watercolours of alpine subjects, formerly in the Elmhirst collections are *View down the Val d'Aosta* (Private collection, Wilton 1432), *An Alpine Valley* (Museum of Fine Arts, Boston, Wilton 1451) and *A Mountain Gorge* (Museum of Art, Rhode Island School of Design, Wilton 1453)

IAN WARRELL

SAMUEL PALMER 1805–1881

An illustration to Milton's 'Lycidas'

Watercolour over pencil, heightened with
scratching out and gouache
4⅛ × 6 inches · 104 × 151 mm
Signed 'S Palmer' (lower left)
Painted c.1864–1870

COLLECTIONS
Alexander Campbell Blair, Conway, (d.1935);
Thomas George McGill Duncan MC;
Niall McGill Duncan, to 1976;
Robert Tear, 2011;
And by descent, 2014.

LITERATURE
Raymond Lister (ed.), *The Letters of Samuel
Palmer*, vol.II, Oxford, 1974, p.691;
Arnold Fawcus *et al.*, *Samuel Palmer: A Vision
Recaptured: The Complete Etchings and the
Paintings for Milton and for Virgil*, London,
1978, p.35;
Raymond Lister, *Catalogue raisonné of the
Works of Samuel Palmer,* Cambridge, 1988,
p.218, M7.

EXHIBITED
London, Victoria & Albert Museum, *A Vision
Recaptured*, 1978, no.XVI (b).

This small, intense and exquisitely executed
watercolour was made by Palmer as a
preparatory study for one of the grandest of his Miltonic watercolours, *Lycidas*,
which he exhibited at the Society of
Painters in Water Colour in 1873. The
composition reprised one of Palmer's most
beloved motifs, the ploughman working
at the opening of the day. The innovative
combination of techniques – Palmer has
used watercolour, gouache on a prepared
board heightened with scratching out – to
create an immediate and lyrical composition which is diluted in the larger finished
watercolour. Palmer's Miltonic watercolours represent the triumph of his later
career, marking a return to many of the
ideas about landscape which characterised
his Shoreham period works.

Palmer was fascinated by Milton
throughout his life but only embarked
upon his large-scale cycle of illustrations
after securing the patronage of the Leonard
Rowe Valpy. In 1863 Valpy acquired Palmer's
Twilight – The Chapel by the Bridge and after
asking Palmer to alter certain aspects of the
watercolour he asked the artist if he had
anything: 'in hand which specially affected
his 'inner sympathies.'[1] Palmer replied to
Valpy:
*I carried the Minor Poems in my pocket for
twenty years, and once of designs for* L'Allegro
and Il Penseroso, *not one of which I have
painted(!!!), though I have often made and
sold other subjects from subjects (not however
monotonous in their shape yet still a set;
perhaps a dozen or so), half from the one and
half from the other poem. For I never artisti-
cally know 'such a sacred and homefelt delight'
as when endeavouring in all humility, so realize
after a sort of imagery of Milton.*[2]

Samuel Palmer
Illustration to Milton's 'Lycidas'
Watercolour over pencil heightened with gouache, gum
arabic and scratching out · 15½ × 23 inches · 395 × 584 mm
Signed and inscribed
Private collection · Photograph courtesy of Sotheby's

Samuel Palmer
The Early Ploughman
Etching · 7⅛ × 10 inches · 180 × 252 mm
© The Trustees of the British Museum

Valpy commissioned eight watercolours in total – three from *L'Allegro* and five from *Il Penseroso* – Palmer took the undertaking extremely seriously and spent some sixteen years on the project producing multiple studies and versions of each composition. Palmer wrote to Valpy in 1879 that: 'I considered your taste and feeling so much above the ordinary standard that, in order fully to satisfy them, I have *lavished time without limit and measure*, even after I myself considered the works complete.'[3] This had the effect of making the Milton works some of the most technically ambitious watercolours he produced, pushing the boundaries of what could be achieved with the medium and producing grand and chromatically bold works.

Palmer's fascination with the Miltonic subjects meant he illustrated scenes from *Comus* and Milton's 1637 pastoral elegy, *Lycidas* as well as *L'Allegro* and *Comus*. The present study illustrates verses from *Lycidas*, inscribed on the verso of the large water–colour:

Together both, ere the high lawns appear'd
Under the opening eye-lids of the morn,
we drove afield, and both together heard
What time the grey-fly winds her sultry horn

The scene depicts a ploughman harnessing his team of oxen under the brilliantly coloured 'opening eye-lids' of the dawn sky and another figure tending to a herd, Lycidas and the narrator of Milton's poem. The setting, with its cypress trees and mountainous hills suggests the Arcadian setting of pastoral poetry, whilst the castle on the hill recalls Palmer's own studies of Harlech Castle.[4] The presence of flocks of birds in the present watercolour recall the 'grey-fly winds' of Milton's verse, a detail omitted in

the larger watercolour. This raises the question of the status of the present work.

Although the large watercolour of Lycidas was not exhibited until 1873 it is likely that our watercolour was made soon after 1864 when Palmer was working out the compositions he was going to paint for Valpy. It is clear from a letter written to the painter George Richmond in 1869 that he was reading and recalling *Lycidas*.[5] Indeed the present study develops a motif Palmer had experimented with in 1861 in an etching entitled *The Early Ploughman*.[6] The idea of rural figures working the land at sunrise appealed to Palmer's deep sympathy with rustic life and the numinous quality of landscape at dawn and dusk. Technically extremely bold in execution, the present watercolour study demonstrates Palmer's extraordinary ability at communicating a powerfully beatific vision of rural labour on a miniature scale.

NOTES

1   Raymond Lister, *Catalogue Raisonné of the works of Samuel Palmer*, Cambridge, 1988, p.8.
2   Ed. Raymond Lister, *The Letters of Samuel Palmer*, Oxford, 1974, II, p.691.
3   Ed. Raymond Lister, *The Letters of Samuel Palmer*, Oxford, 1974, II, p.965.
4   Raymond Lister, *Catalogue Raisonné of the works of Samuel Palmer*, Cambridge, 1988, nos.267 and 269.
5   Ed. Raymond Lister, *The Letters of Samuel Palmer*, Oxford, 1974, II,p.806.
6   Will Vaughan, *Samuel Palmer 1805–1881: Vision and Landscape*, exh.cat., London (British Museum), 2005, no.140, pp.219–220.

SIMEON SOLOMON 1840–1905

Queen Esther hearing the news of the intended massacre of the Jews

Pen and ink with some lead white
on paper laid to board (the main sheet with
three narrow additions)
11¼ × 13¾ inches · 285 × 350 mm
Signed with monogram and dated
10 / 10 / [18]60

COLLECTIONS
James Leathart, Newcastle, 1895;
Robert Isaacson;
James Draper, New York, 2014.

LITERATURE
Simon Reynolds, *The Vision of Simeon
Solomon*, London, 1985, plate 20;
Colin Cruise, *et al.*, *Love Revealed: Simeon
Solomon and the Pre-Raphaelites*, exh.cat.,
Birmingham (Birmingham Museum and Art
Gallery), 2005, pp.48, 82, 97, 104.

EXHIBITED
London, Goupil Gallery, Adolphe Goupil
and W. M. Rossetti, *Pre-Raphaelite Collection:
D. G. Rossetti, Ford Madox Brown, Holman
Hunt, Burne-Jones, Albert Moore, Simeon
Solomon, Inchbold*; June–July 1896, no.23;
Birmingham, Museum and Art Gallery,
Munich, Museum Villa Stuck & London,
Ben Uri Art Gallery, *Love Revealed: Simeon
Solomon and the Pre-Raphaelites*, 2005–6,
no.47.

This major early drawing by Simeon Solomon depicts the Jewish Queen Esther hearing the news that her Persian husband King Ahasuerus plans to massacre the Jews living in his kingdom. Ahasuerus had been advised by Haman, Esther's enemy, who knew that she was Jewish and would be unable to avoid the decree; Solomon focusses on the moment she hears the news, exploring her considerations of personal grief and the wider tragedy of her race. The intricate and highly finished drawing reflects the influence of Dante Gabriel Rossetti on Solomon's earliest work. Carefully executed in pen and ink, this drawing is typical of Solomon's earliest style reflecting his affinity with the previous generation of Pre-Raphaelites and his interest in scenes from Jewish history.

Simeon Solomon trained as a painter in his brother's studio and at F. S. Cary's academy until his admission to the Royal Academy Schools in 1856; he made his début at the Royal Academy in 1857 at the age of seventeen. Solomon rapidly became identified with the Pre-Raphaelites through his friendship with Dante Gabriel Rossetti and Edward Burne-Jones although his closeness to Algernon Charles Swinburne from 1863 was to be more significant, strengthening his ties to Pre-Raphaelite poetry and offering new, highly controversial subject matter. Rossetti's influence is clearly apparent both in the subject matter and technique of Solomon's watercolours of the late 1850s and early 1860s particularly in complex drawings such his depiction of *Queen Esther*. Solomon has densely worked the sheet with surface detail, in a similar manner to Rossetti's drawings from this date. For example the highly finished drawing of *Sir Launcelot*

in the Queen's Chamber in the Birmingham Museum and Art Gallery drawn in 1857 which shows Guinevere at a moment of intense personal crisis, her infidelity with Sir Launcelot having been discovered.[1] Rossetti shows Guinevere standing with her hands clasped looking in despair surrounded by her female attendants who are weeping at the plight of their mistress providing an obvious visual source for Solomon's treatment of Queen Esther.

The subject-matter may have been prompted by a project Solomon was involved in to provide illustrations to the Bible. Along with several notable artists in the Pre-Raphaelite circle, Solomon was commissioned by the Dalziel brothers to produce drawings for their projected illustrated Bible, for which he was allocated twenty subjects. The project was never completed, although the illustrations appeared in Dalziel's Bible Gallery published in 1880 with narrative captions.[2] In the present drawing Solomon has captured the description of the king's palace from *The Book of Esther* (1:16) as Colin Cruise has pointed out is also inspired by the excavations at Ninevah and the contemporary vogue for Pre-Raphaelite historical fidelity first put forward by Ford Madox Brown in his essay 'On the Mechanism of a Historical Picture', published in *The Gem* in February 1850.[3] The furniture Solomon depicts, for example, appears to have been derived from William Holman Hunt's designs of *c.*1855, made by J. G. Crace.

This striking and meticulously finished drawing neatly represents Solomon's early career, when he was most under the influence of Rossetti. The drawing, with its boldly delineated figures, seen against a

Dante Gabriel Rossetti (1828–1882)
Sir Launcelot in the Queen's Chamber, 1857
Pen and ink and watercolour on paper
10¼ × 13¾ inches · 260 × 350 mm
Birmingham Museums and Art Gallery / Bridgeman Images

background of surface detail, also recalls Solomon's interest in graphic design, particularly his engravings for the Dalziel Bible Gallery and work designing stained glass windows for William Morris. In exceptionally fine condition, this drawing is both an important early work by Solomon and an exceptional, late Pre-Raphaelite work.

NOTES

1   Virginia Surtees, *Dante Gabriel Rossetti 1828–1882 The Paintings and Drawings: A Catalogue Raisonné*, Oxford, 1975, p.54, no.95.
2   Colin Cruise, *Love Revealed: Simeon Solomon and the Pre-Raphaelites*, exh.cat., London, Birmingham Museum & Art Gallery, 2005, pp.13–21.
3   Colin Cruise, *Love Revealed: Simeon Solomon and the Pre-Raphaelites*, exh.cat., London, Birmingham Museum & Art Gallery, 2005, no.47, p.97.

Sir William Agnew 1825–1910: 'The Grand Mogul of picture-trade-land'[1]

Harry Furniss (1854–1925)
Sir William Agnew, 1st Bt, 1880s
Pen and ink · 8⅛ × 6⅝ inches · 205 × 168 mm
© National Portrait Gallery, London

William Agnew was one of the greatest art dealers of the nineteenth century. Born in Salford in 1825 he was the second son of Thomas Agnew, the founder of Thos. Agnew & Sons the art dealers, based initially in Manchester. William Agnew moved the centre of activity to London in 1860 and the firm rapidly became one of the major forces in the international trade in old master paintings. Agnew was responsible for helping to form some of the greatest collections of the second half of the nineteenth century in both Britain and America, his clients included Cornelius Vanderbilt, Meyer A. Rothschild, Nathaniel de Rothschild, Baron Ferdinand de Rothschild – who purchased many of his greatest eighteenth-century

British paintings from Agnew – George Salting, Sir Arthur Bass, Lord Faringdon, Sir Henry Tate, Sir Charles Tennant and Sir Edward Guinness, 1st Earl of Iveagh. It was Iveagh who would make the most spectacular collection, entirely purchased from Agnew's, he bequeathed it in part to the nation, along with a fine Robert Adam villa in Hampstead, Kenwood House. Of the 63 pictures in the Iveagh collection at Kenwood, 62 came from Agnew's and were largely purchased between June 1887 and April 1891. William Agnew forged a dealing model and reputation which is comparable to that of Joseph Duveen a generation later. But unlike Duveen, Agnew's also sold many contemporary artists and forged a close relationship with John Millais, Frederic Leighton, Edward Burne-Jones and actively supported both Frank Holl and the sculptor Ford Onslow Ford whose portraits of Agnew are offered here.

In 1840 William Agnew joined his father as an apprentice in the gallery, which had been based in Exchange Street in Manchester since 1826. The firm traded chiefly in British contemporary artists such as Daniel Maclise, J. R. Herbert, and Clarkson Stanfield. This profile gradually changed and from the move to London – initially in Waterloo Place and from 1875 at purpose built premises at 39 (now 43) Old Bond Street – William Agnew began to deal more in old master paintings. Agnew's began bidding at Christies on a considerable scale, dominating major sales. For example in 1875 at the sale of the Marlborough gems, Agnew purchased the entire collection with one bid of 35,000 guineas for David Bromilow.[2] Agnew was a great showman who used the public forum of the auction for publicity and to

attract press comment and new clients to his London gallery. In 1876, shortly after the completion of the new gallery in Bond Street, Agnew purchased at the Wynn Ellis sale at Christie's, Gainsborough's portrait of *Georgiana, Duchess of Devonshire* for 10,100 guineas. Then a world record price for a picture sold at auction. Agnew also bid on behalf of clients, including the National Gallery, purchasing William Hogarth's *Shrimp Girl* and *Lavinia Fenton, Duchess of Bolton* from the Leigh Court sale in 1884. An account of the sale in 1890 of the collection of William Wells gives a sense of Agnew's charismatic and theatrical presence in the saleroom:

Christie's was crammed full on the Saturday afternoon, though the sale could have been conducted quite well in a four-wheeled cab, for Mr. Agnew bought nearly everything. Roughly speaking, he spent nearly £50,000 out of £77,000 which the sale produced. After the sale was over he might have been seen contemplating a sixpenny butting-hole in a Piccadilly flower shop as cool as a cucumber... They make a mighty bother about Stanley's cap, but Barnum certainly ought also to secure Mr. Agnew's caput-coverer. You can't see Mr Agnew's jovial countenance, you can't hear Agnew's formidable voice, but that hat of his holds you like the eye of an ancient mariner. Every bob of that hat means a thousand. It is splendid.[3]

Contemporary painters also benefited from Agnew's auction activities. The Wells sale comprised principally British nineteenth-century paintings, the centrepiece was a large group of works by Edwin Landseer. Of the 32 canvases by Landseer in the sale, twenty were purchased by Agnew. At the Levy sale in 1876 Agnew bid 6,900 guineas for three pictures by David Cox and 4,220

guineas for three drawings.[4] In 1873 Agnew acquired Holman Hunt's *The Shadow of Death* for the enormous sum of £10,500, then the highest price paid to a an English artist for a painting, the price including the engraving rights. In a single painting show held in the Bond Street gallery Agnew's showed the painting and sold a hugely popular engraving, the success of which largely defrayed the original cost of the picture, enabling Agnew to donate the painting in 1883 to Manchester City Art Gallery.[5] Agnew in turn promoted his client, Sir Henry Tate's ambition to build a National Gallery of British Art.

But it was British pictures of the eighteenth century which represented the most spectacular aspect of Agnew's trade. Baron Ferdinand de Rothschild acquired Gainsborough's *George IV* and Reynolds's *Colonel St. Leger* for £5,750 and Gainsborough's *Pink Boy* for £5,512 and 10 shillings; to Sir Nathaniel de Rothschild, Agnew sold Gainsborough's *The Morning Walk* and Reynolds's *Garrick between Comedy and Tragedy*. It was grand manner portraiture of the late eighteenth century which dominated Lord Iveagh's collection. He acquired fabulous examples by Gainsborough, Reynolds and Romney for the house, along with works by Vermeer and Rembrandt.[6] Agnew became one of the principal dealers in the work of J.M.W. Turner, selling works such as *The Fountain of Indolence*, now in the Beaverbrook Art Gallery, New Brunswick, in 1882 to George W. Vanderbilt; *Rockets and Blue Lights*, now in the Clark Institute, Williamstown, to Sir Julian Goldsmid and in 1887 *Antwerp: Van Goyen Looking out for a subject* to F.B. Henson for £7,507, it would pass in

1901 to the Frick Collection, New York.

Agnew remained friendly with a large circle of contemporary artists whose work he promoted and sold in large numbers. There was a list hanging in the front saloon of the Bond Street gallery on which customers could put their name down for 'the next Peter Graham but three'![7] Agnew supplied the taste for landscapes by John Linnell, David Roberts, Vicat Cole and William Müller and subject-pictures by Frederick Leighton, Edwin Long, William Orchardson and Alma Tadema. Agnew was also proprietor of the magazine *Punch* which brought him into contact with numerous artists and illustrators, including George du Maurier and particularly John Tenniel, who became a very great friend. Agnew commissioned Frank Holl to paint Tenniel in 1883, a picture he bequeathed to the National Gallery. Agnew as the pre-eminent figure in the commercial art world was naturally the subject of a number of portraits by the artists he knew and supported. William Agnew epitomized the commercial and social success possible to entrepreneurs in late Victorian England. His activities as a picture dealer created a new model for an international art market as well as great personal wealth. His securely established position enabled him, a supporter of Gladstone, to sit as an MP for South East Lancashire between 1880 and 1885, the year in which he was created a Baronet. His purchase of the sporting and agricultural estate of Rougham in Suffolk in 1904 further underlined his commercial success.

Described by a contemporary as 'the Grand Mogul of picture-trade-land', William Agnew was a hugely important figure in the development of art dealing in the late

nineteenth century. Agnew's carefully cultivated public image and use of the auction rooms for publicity and self-promotion, his international clientele and his cultivation of spectacular clients would form a model for Joseph Duveen a generation later. Like Duveen Agnew was not above sharp practice.[8] But his career stands as a major landmark in the development of the profession and profile of art dealing.

NOTES

1 M. H. Spielmann, 'Glimpses of Artist-life: Christies', *Magazine of Art*, 1888, p.231.

2 John Boardman, *The Marlborough Gems*, Oxford, 2009, pp.17–18.

3 Quoted in Geoffrey Agnew, *Agnew's 1817–1967*, London, 1967, p.38.

4 See Scott Wilcox, *Sun, Wind, and Rain: The Art of David Cox*, exh.cat., New Haven (Yale Centre for British Art), 2009, pp.58–61.

5 Judith Bronkhurst, *William Holman Hunt: A Catalogue Raisonné*, New Haven and London, pp.225–228.

6 For the Iveagh Bequest see Julius Bryant, *Kenwood: Paintings in the Iveagh Bequest*, London, 2012.

7 Cited in Geoffrey Agnew, *Agnew's 1817–1967*, London, 1967, p.33.

8 Charles Nugent has pointed out that Agnew used his position as President of the Council of the Whitworth Art Gallery to sell the gallery works Agnew's could not sell elsewhere, Nugent cites a work by George Cattermole purchased at auction in 1889 which he eventually sold to the Whitworth a decade later. See Charles Nugent, *British Watercolours in the Whitworth Art Gallery, The University of Manchester*, Manchester, 2003, p.11.

SIR FRANK HOLL RA 1845–1888

Sir William Agnew, 1st Bt (1825–1910)

Oil on canvas
25¾ × 22 inches · 654 × 559 mm
In the original Watts style frame
Painted in 1883

COLLECTIONS
Sir William Agnew;
Walter Agnew, son of the above;
Colonel Richard Leslie Agnew, son of the
above;
Thos. Agnew & Sons, purchased from the
above, 17 May 1956;
Thomas Agnew & Sons, to 2013.

LITERATURE
Geoffrey Agnew, *Agnew's 1817–1967*, London,
1967, repr. p.31;
R. Tremble, *Great Victorian Pictures: their
Paths to Fame*, exh.cat., London (Arts Council
of Great Britain), 1978, p.44;

Frank Holl
Sir John Tenniel, c.1883
Oil on canvas · 23¾ × 18¾ inches · 603 mm × 476 mm
© National Portrait Gallery, London
Bequeathed by Sir William Agnew, 1st Bt, 1911

Giles Waterfield, *Art Treasures of England*,
exh.cat., London (Royal Academy of Arts),
1998, no.16.

EXHIBITED
London, Thos. Agnew and Sons,
*Loan Exhibition of Victorian Painting
1837–1887*, 1961, no.12;
London, Royal Academy, *Art Treasures
of England*, 1998, no.16.

Frank Holl is best known for his genre
paintings, but he was celebrated by contemporaries as a portraitists. In 1879 he exhibited
at the Royal Academy a portrait of the
engraver Samuel Cousins which caused a
sensation and until his death in 1888 he painted a further 197 portraits of many political
and society figures, Holl's output reflected
the internationalism of the art market by
the end of the nineteenth century, one of his
last sitter's being the great New York banker
and collector J. Pierpont Morgan, Holl's
portrait is now in the Morgan Library and
Art Gallery. Morgan in-turn acquired a great
deal of material through Sir William Agnew.
Holl was a close friend of Sir William
Agnew, a fact testified to by their volumi-
nous correspondence. Agnew was an early
promoter of Holl's work; Holl's daughter,
A.M. Reynolds, describing him as one of
her father's 'dearest friends and staunchest
admirers.'[1] Agnew was Secretary of the
Frank Holl Memorial Trust set up after Holl's
death; the Trust succeeded in erecting a
monument in St Paul's. Agnew frequently
bought and sold Holl's works, he acquired
the *Seamstresses*, now in the collection of the
Royal Albert Memorial Museum, Exeter, at
auction in 1889 for 285 guineas and sold it in
turn to one of his greatest clients Sir Charles

Tennant. Agnew commissioned a portrait
of the artist Sir John Tenniel in 1883. Tenniel
worked as a cartoonist at *Punch* where he
formed a friendship with Agnew, its part-
proprietor. The portrait remained with
Agnew until his death, when he bequeathed
it to the National Gallery. In 1887 Agnew
helped initiate Holl's commission to paint
a portrait of the great Liberal politician
and former Prime Minister, William Ewart
Gladstone. Gladstone was then Leader of
the Opposition and the portrait was painted
at Hawarden his estate in Flintshire, it was
seen by Agnew in progress; Holl wrote to his
wife that Agnew was in 'the most wild state
of enthusiasm over it.'[2]

It was in the same year that Agnew commissioned the portrait of Tenniel, that he sat to
Holl himself. The present highly fluid and
incisive portrait study was made in preparation for a three-quarter length portrait which
Holl exhibited at the Royal Academy in 1883.
The rapidly executed portrait is typical of
Holl's work and his sketchy brushwork bears
comparison with his fashionable French
contemporary, Charles-Émile-Auguste
Carolus-Duran. Despite the apparent speed
of execution, the highly finished head offers
a powerful and extremely revealing character study of one of Holl's most important
supporters.

*We are grateful to Mark Bills for his help in
preparing this entry.*

NOTES

1   A. M. Reynolds, *The Life and Work of Frank
Holl*, London, 1912, p.226.
2   Ed. Mark Bills, *Frank Holl: Emerging from the
Shadows*, exh.cat. Guildford (Watts Gallery),
2013, p.155.

EDWARD ONSLOW FORD RA 1852–1901

Sir William Agnew, 1st Bt (1825–1910)

Marble, on a square yellow marble socle
Height: 30 inches; 762 mm, overall
Signed and dated: 'E Onslow Ford / 1898'
(to reverse)

COLLECTIONS
By descent in the firm of Thos. Agnew &
Sons, London until 2013.

EXHIBITED
London, Royal Academy of Arts, 1899
(2015).

John McLure Hamilton (1853-1936)
Edward Onslow Ford, 1893
Oil on canvas · 17½ × 23½ inches; 445 × 597 mm
© National Portrait Gallery, London
Given by John McLure Hamilton, 1920, NPG 1866

This notable bust of Sir William Agnew was executed by the sculptor Edward Onslow Ford shortly after Agnew's retirement from the firm which he had propelled to pre-eminence. The portrait is a penetrating study of Agnew, displaying Ford's extra-ordinary ability to render a likeness. The bust was exhibited at the Royal Academy in 1899 and then was displayed permanently in Agnew's imposing purpose-built premises at 39 (now 43) Old Bond Street.

Ford's first public commission, a bronze statue of Sir Rowland Hill was soon followed by a life-sized marble portrait of Sir Henry Irving as Hamlet now in the Guildhall Art Gallery, London. From 1884 Ford came into close contact with Alfred Gilbert, who occupied a neighbouring studio in The Avenue, Fulham Road. Thanks to what Gilbert characterised as Ford's 'powers of assimilation', his work began to reflect Gilbert's style and approach.[1] Ford assisted Gilbert in his experiments with lost-wax casting, and went on to establish his reputation with statuettes in this medium.

Ford's art related closely to the arts and crafts movement – he was a founder member of the Art Workers' Guild in 1884 particularly when and where it crossed traditional boundaries between sculpture and precious metalwork. He was the first British New Sculptor to exhibit mixed-media works, and was thus an important precursor to George Frampton, William Reynolds-Stephens, and Gilbert Bayes. Ford's earliest and best-known work of this type is *The Singer*.[2] This bronze statuette portrays an Egyptian girl wearing turquoises and garnets in her circlet, holding a harp decorated with imitation enamelling. Ford's

masterpiece is his memorial to Percy Bysshe Shelley, the most ambitious Victorian figure sculpture in Oxford. Originally intended for the protestant cemetery in Rome, it proved too large for its site. Following its acclaim at the 1892 Royal Academy, it was accepted by University College, Oxford, where Shelley had briefly been an undergraduate.

The contemporary writer on sculpture Marion Spielmann admired Ford's portrait busts as much as his ideal sculptures: 'they are speaking likenesses: in every instance the man himself (or the lady) is before you.'[3] Though Ford was less prolific in this area than Edgar Boehm and Thomas Brock, his busts surpassed theirs in sympathy towards their sitters' personalities and in vividness of modelling. This is particularly evident in the bust of Agnew which is rendered with extraordinary naturalism down to his facial blemishes. The directness of the portrait of Agnew is off-set by the grandeur of its conception; Ford has deliberately left the underside of the bust roughly carved suggesting the original marble block and recalling the work of Michelangelo. The conceit of the unfinished block also makes the bust appear like a fragment. The portrait is finished with a yellow marble socle, adding an element of polychromy a particular feature of Ford's works.

NOTES
1 Isabel McAllister, *Alfred Gilbert*, London, 1924, p.94.
2 Ed. Martina Droth. *Sculpture Victorious: Art in the Age of Invention, 1837–1901*, exh.cat., New Haven (Yale Center for British Art), 2014, pp.383-387.
3 Marion Spielmann, *British Sculpture and Sculptors of Today*, London, 1901, p.63.

JOHN BRATBY RA 1928–1992

Kitchen Interior with Jean and David

Black chalk and crayon on four sheets of
paper
66 × 42½ inches · 1675 × 1080 mm
Executed *c*.1957–8

COLLECTIONS
Julian Hartnoll, London;
Stanley Seeger and Christopher Cone,
to 2014.

LITERATURE
Julian Hartnoll, *John Bratby 1928 – 1992*,
exh.cat., London, 2003, no.9, repr. p.9;
Maurice Yacowar, *The Great Bratby: a Portrait
of John Bratby*, London, 2008, p.53, repr.

EXHIBITED
London, Julian Hartnoll, *John Bratby 1928 –
1992*, Spring 2003, no.9.

*Interior with Jean and David is a kitchen drama
with everything but the sink.*[1]

This masterly drawing by John Bratby depicting his wife, the painter Jean Cooke and two
year old son David, amongst the domestic
clutter of a kitchen, encapsulates a form of
social realism practiced by a number of young
artists in the 1950s who were described as
'kitchen sink' painters. An unusually ambitious
composition made up of four sheets of paper
and measuring over 5 feet in height, the drawing demonstrates Bratby's fascination with the
minutiae of everyday life. Made at the height
of his critical and commercial success, this
bold drawing stands as a remarkable testament
to the aims and objectives of the artists who
exhibited at the Beaux Arts Gallery in the late
1950s and demonstrates what the critic and
cultural historian John Berger noted was their
reaction: 'against Style … as a dishonest keeping up of attitudes or appearances.'[2]

Berger's review, which ascribed a strong
political and social message to Bratby's paintings, suggested that they: 'abound with full-
blooded affirmation, celebrating the quick as
against the dead, pleasure and pain as against
oblivion' adding his intensity 'disregards all
conventions of self-consciousness or dignity.'

Bratby was trained at the Royal College of
Art, where he met fellow student Jean Cooke
whom he married in April 1954. The same year
Bratby had the first of a series of one-man
exhibitions at the acclaimed Beaux Arts Gallery,
and his public career was launched. With his
trademark thick paint and his flair for publicity
(he had a talent for leaking stories to the press),
Bratby soon became not only a folk hero in the
art schools of Britain, but a household name.
At first the critics' response was overwhelm-
ingly supportive, with the *Sunday Times*

John Bratby
Susan Ballam, 1956
Pencil on paper · 52 × 19½ inches ·1321 × 495 mm
Tate, London, presented by Sir Edward and Lady Hulton
© The estate of John Bratby.
All Rights Reserved 2010 / Bridgeman Art Library

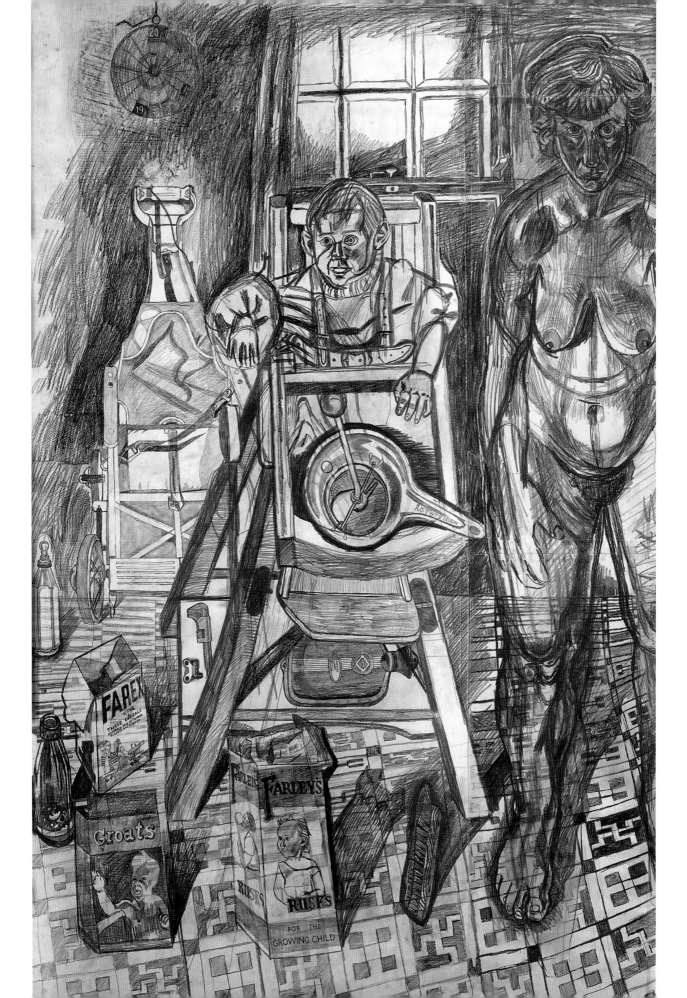

FAREX

Groats

FARLEYS

FARLEYS

RUSKS

RUSKS

FOR THE
GROWING CHILD

Bratby painting in the kitchen at Blackheath with Jean and David.
The Bratby Archive courtesy of Julian Hartnoll

John Bratby
Jean and Still Life in Front of a Window, 1954
Oil on board · 48 × 42½ inches · 1200 × 1080 mm
Southampton City Art Gallery, Hampshire, UK /
John Bratby Estate by courtesy of Julian Hartnoll /
Bridgeman Images

comparing Bratby's rendition of a cornflake packet favourably with Velázquez's Rokeby Venus. A major early painting, Still-Life with Chip Frier, was purchased by the Tate Gallery in 1956.

The term 'kitchen sink realism' was first used by David Sylvester in a review of the Beaux Arts Quartet. Writing in *Encounter* in December 1954 he noted that their work: 'takes us back from the studio to the kitchen' and described their subjects as: 'an inventory which includes every kind of food and drink, every utensil and implement, the usual plain furniture and even babies' nappies on the line. Everything but the kitchen sink? The kitchen sink too.' Sylvester also emphasised that these kitchens were ones 'in which ordinary people cooked ordinary food and doubtless lived their ordinary lives.'[3] The term as it was initially applied to the work of Bratby, Derrick Greaves, Edward Middleditch and Jack Smith, was meant satirically and rejected by the artists themselves. But it soon had traction in describing their paintings of and more widely to characterise plays, novels and films whose working class protagonists railed against the banality of domestic convention. Kitchen sink drama was most famously embodied by John Osborne in his play *Look Back in Anger* of 1956, the publicity for which in-turn coined the term 'Angry young men', but it was Sylvester's description of Bratby's paintings which has definitively described this cultural movement. Kitchen Sink reached its apogee in 1956 when the Beaux Arts Quartet were selected to represent Britain at the Venice Biennale.

Bratby's powerful drawing precisely crystallises this moment in British art. This kitchen scene executed with an expressionistic power suggests the new social realism praised by Berger. Jean Cooke is seen standing amongst the domestic clutter of the kitchen; as with other compositions of the period, such as *Jean and Still Life in Front of a Window*, now in Southampton City Art Gallery, Bratby depicts her naked. At the centre of the composition is their son, David, seated in his highchair with a baby mouli prominently placed on its tray. Bratby has deliberately altered the perspective to reveal the interior of the mouli with its handle and blade. On the floor are a number of packages of familiar children's food – Farley's rusks, Groats and Farex – along with a child's bottle; the linoleum floor itself is a carefully drawn mosaic of geometric shapes. The ambitious, boldly drawn, black chalk composition echoes Bratby's technique as a painter, with areas of deep shadow achieved by heavy working. Whether Bratby was conscious of the social and political ambitions ascribed by commentators such as Berger, his work was designed as a rejection of contemporary British art; his realism was seen as more egalitarian than both the neo-romanticism of John Piper and John Minton and the abstractions of Ben Nicholson.[4] Whilst it was rapidly overshadowed by American abstract expressionism and pop art, Bratby and the other Kitchen Sink realists represented an important, if brief moment, in post-war British art and the present powerful drawing is perfect distillation of these ideas.

NOTES

1   Maurice Yacowar, *The Great Bratby: A Portrait of John Bratby*, London, 2008, p.53.
2   John Berger, 'John Bratby', *New Statesman and Nation*, 25 September 1954, p.358.
3   Quoted in Maurice Yacowar, *The Great Bratby: A Portrait of John Bratby*, London, 2008, p.31.
4   Larry Berrymen, 'The Kitchen Sink Painters', *Arts Review*, 5 April 1991, p.170.

LOWELL
LIBSON LTD
BRITISH ART

Lowell Libson Ltd specialises in British art with an emphasis on paintings, watercolours, drawings and sculpture of the seventeenth to mid-nineteenth centuries. We count many leading North American, European and British museums and private collectors amongst our clients.

Lowell Libson has over thirty-five years experience in dealing. Formerly he was a director of Leger Galleries and Managing Director of Spink-Leger Pictures. He is a member of the organising committee of *Master Drawings & Sculpture London,* a member of the executive committee of the *Society of London Art Dealers* and the *Walpole Society* and in 2011 was appointed a member of the *Reviewing Committee on the Export of Works of Art and Objects of Cultural Interest.* The gallery's research is led by Jonny Yarker who recently completed a PhD at the University of Cambridge and has a considerable reputation as a scholar of British painting and the Grand Tour. He has published

widely and held academic fellowships in America, London, and most recently, Rome. Day to day management of the gallery is in the hands of Deborah Greenhalgh who has long and valuable experience in the art market.

Lowell Libson Ltd actively supports art historical research in Britain and America. The gallery has mounted a number of important loan exhibitions including *Masterpieces of English Watercolours & Drawings* from the National Gallery of Scotland and works by Thomas Rowlandson drawn from British private collections. Lowell Libson Ltd. have sponsored a number of exhibitions including: *Thomas Gainsborough's Landscapes* at the Holburne Museum, Bath, 2011; *Constable Gainsborough Turner and the Making of Landscape* at the Royal Academy, 2012. In 2014 sponsored the Wright of Derby exhibition at the Holburne Museum and supported *A Dialogue with Nature* at the Morgan Library, New York.

We believe that the process of acquiring a work of art should be an enjoyable and stimulating experience and have created a gallery that offers clients the opportunity to discuss and view pictures in discreet and comfortable surroundings. We act as both principals and agents in the purchase and sale of works of art giving clients great flexibility and choice. We offer advice on all aspects of collecting pictures. This includes the purchase and sale of works of art as well as conservation, restoration, framing, lighting and hanging. The gallery also provides a complete curatorial service for collections. Visitors are always welcome at the gallery, which operates on a 'by appointment' basis, to view pictures or to discuss their collections.

LOWELL LIBSON LTD
3 Clifford Street · London w1s 2lf
Telephone: +44 (0)20 7734 8686
Email: pictures@lowell-libson.com
Website: www.lowell-libson.com